SILK ROA

CW00448753

SILK ROAD PILGRIMAGE

PILGRIM DAVID

Copyright © 2012 Pilgrim David

Published in 2012 by Wide Margin,
90 Sandyleaze, Gloucester, GL2 0PX, UK

http://www.wide-margin.co.uk/

The right of Pilgrim David to be identified as the Author of this Work has been asserted by him in accordance
with the Copyright, Designs and Patents Act 1988

*All rights reserved. No part of this publication may be
reproduced, stored in a retrieval system, or transmitted in any
form or by any means electronic, or mechanical, photocopying,
recording or otherwise, without the prior permission of the
publisher or a licence permitting restricted copying.*

ISBN 978-0-9565943-5-8

Printed and bound in Great Britain by
Lightning Source, Milton Keynes

CONTENTS

A NOTE ON TRANSLATIONS

Travelling along the Great Silk Road, one meets people speaking many different languages. Many of the languages are Turkic ones (e.g. Uighur, Kazak, Uzbek and Azeri) but there are also Iranian languages such as Tajik and some peoples who speak languages related to Mongolian or to Chinese. In the Caucasus region there are many different languages, some of which, like Georgian, seem to be unique to the Caucasus and do not have clear links with languages outside of that region. Although I can speak a little Chinese and Turkish, and in the past have also studied some basic Tatar and Mongolian, the language that today usually still serves as a common language for travellers in countries such as Kyrgyzstan, Uzbekistan, Turkmenistan or Azerbaijan is actually Russian. It is not my own native language, nor the language of my friends in these countries, but it was the common language that my friends and I both knew and that we could use to converse with one another. Therefore the conversations recorded in this book are usually translations from Russian, occasionally from Chinese or another language.

However, if we spoke about spiritual topics, my friends were usually more familiar with the names of prophets as these are expressed in their own native language. For instance, they may have heard of the prophet 'Musa' (Мұса), and even know people with that name nowadays, but the Russian name 'Moisey' (Моисей) or the English form 'Moses' may sound strange to them. Actually, all of these are derived ultimately from the ancient Hebrew name מֹשֶׁה (mō·šeh) that in modern Hebrew is *Moshe* but in the course of transmission from one language to another the names have become a little changed. Often the names have not come directly from their original Hebrew forms but have been transmitted via another language, such as Syriac, Arabic or even Turkish, before it reached the peoples of Central Asia, just as in Europe they came via Greek or Latin. On the way, the pronunciation may be altered a little according to the features of the various different languages.

That is why I preferred to use the local forms of these names when I was speaking with people, so that they would understand that I was not talking about a 'foreign' prophet but one that was already familiar to them, whose name they already knew. Out of respect for the local cultures, I prefer to keep these local words in the text of this translation rather than using the English forms. Similarly, I have tried to avoid even using the Russian forms of words if there is a local equivalent: for example, it is common in English to use the forms 'Kazakh' and 'Kazakhstan' but these are actually transliterations of the Russian terms Казах and Казахстан rather than being based on the Kazak terms *Қазақ* and *Қазақстан*. By deliberately using the local terms, my aim is to help to keep the *local* context in the mind of the reader and to emphasise the need to understand *local* cultures, using *local* terms if these are more familiar to the *local* people.

Of course, in a region as wide as Central Asia there are also regional differences. In some places people may have heard of a prophet named in their language Ibrahim or Ibrakhim, but in other places he is called Ibragim. Even in places where they say 'Ibragim', however, they usually recognise the term 'Ibrahim' but may not be familiar with the versions of this name in Russian (Авраам – Avraam) or English (Abraham).

If names of people can sometimes be difficult to translate from one language to another, it is much more of a challenge to translate concepts and ideas, especially when these involve spiritual topics to do with God or eternity. A word in one language may have a range of nuances which may be translated by a variety of different words in another language. That is why a friend of mine from the North Caucasus (from the Karachai people) who took me to an Islamic bookshop in Nalchik recommended one translation of the Qur'an into Russian rather than another one.

In such cases, it is actually good to be able to compare different versions to get a clearer idea of the intended meaning. I have the same problem in this book when quoting from holy writings that were originally written in Hebrew or Greek and have been translated into English. Sometimes one translation seems to be clearer than another. I have indicated in the footnotes which translation I was using. Often I used the New International Version (published in 1978 by the International Bible Society; the first British edition was published by Hodder and Stoughton, London, Sydney and Auckland, in 1979) but sometimes I have also used the NET Bible available on the Internet (http://net.bible.org), published between 1996 and 2006 by Biblical Studies Press, L.L.C.

In using one or the other translation I am not claiming that one is in any way 'better' than the other overall but I have chosen the one that seems to express the meaning in clearer English or else is closer to the Russian version I was also using. I have taken the liberty of replacing the 'English' forms of certain names with their 'Central Asian' forms and in choosing the appropriate 'Central Asian' terms I have usually followed the forms used in the 'Eastern' version of the Russian scriptures – the title in Russian being Священное Писание

– Смысловой перевод Таурата, Книги Пророков, Забура и Инжила (Издательство «Стамбул», Атаскадеро, 2003).

However, where that translation uses the term Иса Масих (Isa Masikh) I have used instead the form 'Isa Mesih' which is the term used in modern Turkey (except that Turkish has a dot over the capital I) and is also very close to the terms used in various local languages of Central Asia and the Caucasus. This great prophet is called in Azeri *İsa Məsih*, in Karakalpak *Ийса Масих*, in Kazak *Иса Мәсix*, in Kyrgyz *Ыйса Машайак*, in Tajik *Исои Масех*, in Uighur *Әйса Масиһ* and in Uzbek *Исо Масиҳ*. I do not think it really matters which name we use because 'Mesih' is actually a title, meaning 'Anointed One'—referring to anointing as a sign of the special ministry given to prophets, priests and kings. The name 'Isa' is derived from the Hebrew name 'Yeshua', a shortened form of 'Yehoshua', which means 'Salvation from the Lord'—that is (in other words), 'God's Salvation'. His name was actually chosen by God himself, who said that the child was to be called by this name because he would save his people from their sins.[1]

PREFACE

Since my first visit to Uzbekistan in 1982, I have fallen in love with the people of Central Asia. More than a quarter of a century has elapsed since then and there have been many external changes in the region. However, the hearts of the people have remained warm and hospitable. In the face of economic or other difficulties, many people are sincerely trying to live life in the best way they can, in honesty and truth. I greatly respect the sincerity of their hearts and their desire to know what is real, what is true and what is worthy of emulation.

This book shares some of my conversations with people of Central Asia. I have been privileged to share in their lives, enjoying the warmth of their hospitality and the richness of their culture. I have learned many things from them, especially some of their values of hospitality, generosity and kindness. This book is a reflection of my appreciation for the values and cultures of the peoples of Central Asia.

Sitting around a kitchen table, or travelling together in a bus, at times people have asked me about various important issues in life. Some relate to family matters here and now, such as how to bring up children. (Despite five children of my own, and now two grandchildren, I am still learning how to do this!) Other questions relate to deeper issues in life, such as: 'What is the meaning of life?' or 'Why are we here?' On such topics it might be possible to write many books but still not cover it in depth. Nevertheless, I hope that the selection of conversations, insights and experiences which I am sharing in this book might be of help to some of my friends in Central

Asia and the Caucasus in their own journey on the pilgrimage which is life itself.

Although I am sure that many of my friends would not mind their actual names being published, in some cases, to respect their need for privacy, I have changed the names of some people by giving them different Central Asian names instead. In a few cases, I have refrained from mentioning their names altogether. For the sake of anonymity it has sometimes been necessary to alter a few circumstantial details, such as the location of a conversation, but in essence the discussions and experiences related here reflect ones which have actually taken place with local people in the region. I have also taken the liberty of threading them together into one continuous travelogue rather than keeping them as events on separate journeys. In some cases I have combined together two separate dialogues or have expanded on the content of a particular dialogue so that the overall meaning is clearer—for example, by adding in some extra background information or additional material on that theme. My hope is that these small editorial liberties will be a help rather than a hindrance to the reader who may want to accompany me on my pilgrimage through Central Asia and the Caucasus.

INTRODUCTION

'The Great Silk Road'—what was it? Was it only a trade route (with several variants) along which silk came through Central Asia from China to the Middle East, and various other wares, as well as animals, went eastwards into China? No! Far more important than the material goods was the interaction between different kinds of peoples. All along the Great Silk Road there were people talking with each other, exchanging ideas and sharing aspects of their cultures and traditions.

Religious ideas and practices were also conveyed. In Central Asia many religions lived side by side for centuries. These included not only Islam, Christianity and Buddhism but also lesser-known religions such as Zoroastrianism, Manichaeism and Judaism. In everyday life, however, many people practiced 'folk' religious rituals deriving from 'shamanism', nature worship or ancestral cults. For example, in parts of Central Asia people tie a piece of cloth or a strip of paper to a tree in certain special places as a form of prayer. Where does this custom come from? It is not mentioned in the Qur'an—or even in any *hadith*. In Buryatia I have seen the same practice in a Buddhist context and in Armenia I have seen it near to a church which had been closed up during the Communist period, preventing people from worshipping inside. I have also seen the same practice in Siberia and even in China. It is essentially an offering to the pagan gods or spirits of a locality. For instance, many native peoples of Siberia think that if they go past a sacred place without leaving an offering to the local spirit then the spirit will be angry and could cause something bad to happen. That is why this practice of tying cloths to trees is probably a vestige of shamanism or paganism which then got absorbed into other religions, including Islam, Buddhism and Christianity. Nevertheless people who observe this custom still regard themselves as Muslims, or else as Christians or Buddhists! So in this respect their 'official' religious affiliations are like a superficial paint—but it is not so meaningful if underneath what they actually do or believe is more like paganism or shamanism.

The Great Silk Road has been an important highway for the transmission of religious beliefs and practices all through history. It was one of the doorways through which Buddhism, Christianity and Islam all came into China from Central Asia. The influence of Islam in Central Asia is nowadays so obvious that sometimes people living in the Caucasus, Turkmenistan, Uzbekistan, Kyrgyzstan or northwest China are surprised to learn that many of their ancestors were very likely to have been people who loved Isa Mesih and followed his teachings. In Afghanistan and in the provinces of Xinjiang and Gansu of north-west China their ancestors were possibly Buddhists. Buddhist frescoes at Dunhuang in the Gansu province of China (dating from the 4th to 14th centuries AD) and the huge Buddhist statues at Bamyan in Afghanistan (dating from the 6th century AD)—which were destroyed by the Taliban in 2001—testify to the former influence of Buddhism in areas which nowadays are inhabited mainly by Muslims.[2] Buddhism came into Afghanistan in the third century BC and from there it later went to Xinjiang and Mongolia.[3]

In the same way, the ancestors of many peoples of Central Asia were at one time followers of Isa Mesih. The *Injil* mentions people from Parthia—that is, an area which nowadays includes Iran, Turkmenistan, Tajikistan and parts of Uzbekistan—among those who heard the good news about Isa Mesih about seven weeks after his death and resurrection.[4]

Bartholomew and Thaddaeus—two of those who travelled around with Isa Mesih and who witnessed his resurrection from the dead—later went to the region of what is now Azerbaijan and Armenia, telling people there the good news about Isa Mesih.[5] Two centuries after the birth of Isa Mesih the message came to people now living in southern Dagestan.[6] Right up until the region was annexed by the Russian empire, the Udin people of Azerbaijan preserved their historic identity as followers of Isa Mesih and, having weathered the storm of atheistic Communism, they are now re-discovering the faith of their ancestors.[7]

Meanwhile, from the first century onwards, faith in Isa Mesih had also been spreading to the east of the Caspian Sea, not only throughout the Persian empire but also to India and further east.[8] Faith in Isa Mesih had very deep roots in the region now occupied by Turkmenistan, Uzbekistan, Tajikistan, Kyrgyzstan, Kazakstan and the Uighur regions of China. About two centuries after the birth of Isa Mesih there were already followers of Isa Mesih in Merv (or Mary) in modern Turkmenistan.[9] In subsequent centuries, not only Merv but also Herat in Afghanistan and Bukhara and Samarkand in modern-day Uzbekistan all became important Christian centers.[10] The Samarkand and Bukhara regions, as well as the area that is now Tajikistan, were inhabited by the Sogdian people, among whom were significant numbers of followers of Isa Mesih.[11] As the Sogdians were important traders along the Great Silk Road and travelled extensively into China, Sogdian Christian documents have been found at Bulayïq, near Turfan in Xinjiang.[12] By the time of Chinggis Khan, some of the Mongolian tribes and a number of the Mongolian leaders were also followers of Isa Mesih.[13] As nomads, they were not interested in having permanent religious buildings but instead they recognised that God could be worshipped in any place and in a style which fitted with the local culture.[14] During the Mongol empire and the empires which succeeded it, there continued to be many Christians throughout Central Asia and along the Great Silk Road, from the Caucasus to China and beyond. Historical records mention churches and communities of Christians in places such as Kashgar, now in the Xinjiang province of China; Samarkand, in modern-day Uzbekistan; Khorezm, the region of Uzbekistan around Khiva and Urgench; and Merv in Turkmenistan.[15] Along the Great Silk Road the names on ancient tombstones of those who were followers of Isa Mesih are mainly Turkic ones, with some Persian and other names scattered among them.[16] For example, at Issyk-kul in Kyrgyzstan a tombstone of a follower of Isa Mesih who died in 1312 has an inscription in the Uighur language.[17]

Archaeologists excavating ancient sites along the Great Silk Road continue to find artifacts testifying to the influence of Christianity among the ancestors of today's Uighurs, Kazaks, Kyrgyz, Tajiks, Uzbeks, Turkmen, Azeris and peoples

of the northern Caucasus. The reverence accorded to Isa Mesih by the ancestors of these peoples can be seen in the designs on stone vessels, medallions and other artifacts which are now on display in various museums across the region.[18] This important period in the history of the peoples of Central Asia and the Caucasus had been neglected in the past but it is now being researched and documented by a number of local scholars, including Manarbek Baieke (who is Kazak), Farida Mamedova (who is Azeri) and Rashid Azizov, a Tabassaran scholar from Dagestan.[19]

Even in China, faith in Isa Mesih was also very widespread among the ancestors of the Uighur people, and perhaps also of many Hui (or Dungans as they are known in Kazakstan and Kyrgyzstan). There is evidence that the good news about Isa Mesih was first brought to China in 65 AD by the apostle Thomas, who had personally met with Isa Mesih after his resurrection from the dead; God had even prepared the Emperor of China for this good news by giving the Emperor a dream in which had seen a vision of Isa Mesih.[20] A Chinese scholar named Wang Weifan believes that there is also evidence of Christianity in China as early as 86 AD—that is, within the lifetime of those who had personally witnessed the death of Isa Mesih and his resurrection from the grave.[21] There were definitely followers of Isa Mesih in China by the sixth and seventh centuries AD and by the eighth century they could be found throughout ten provinces of China, with Christian communities in a hundred cities.[22] Information on the followers of Isa Mesih in China at that time is derived from a number of ancient manuscripts but the most famous evidence can be seen on a stele dating from the year 781 which can still be seen in Xi'an, the Chinese city which marks the beginning of the Great Silk Road.[23] Christian manuscripts dated between the seventh and tenth centuries

AD were also preserved in the library of the large Buddhist centre at Dunhuang in Gansu province.[24] By the year 1000 AD there were followers of Isa Mesih right across Central Asia and also in Mongolia, Tibet, India, Burma, Thailand and perhaps further east too.[25]

However, wars and conquests, revolutions, oppression, persecution and the imposition of other ideologies—including atheism during the seventy years of the Soviet Union—have erased many of the externally visible marks of these religions.[26] Nevertheless, inside the hearts of people have been preserved many of the values and beliefs of their ancestors who knew and loved God's Holy Books—including the *Taurat*, *Zabur* and *Injil*. Folk sayings and popular proverbs often preserve some elements of these earlier beliefs. For example, a scholar from the Tabassaran people of Dagestan writes of his own people: "In all Tabassaran settlements, when having a heart-to-heart talk with almost anyone, the traditional spirituality within the ethnic group and in each person is clearly revealed. If one systematises and analyses everything that is said, then by their customs and viewpoints, and also by their conduct, it would be possible to write the Holy Book anew if it were to completely disappear from the face of the earth."[27]

The same author records the impression made on a villager in the mountains of Dagestan who discovered that his own region is also mentioned in the Holy Books: "Even the name of our settlement is reflected in the Bible, in the second book of Kings, chapter seventeen, in the sixth and seventh verses: 'In the ninth year of Hoshea, the king of Assyria captured Samaria and deported the Israelites to Assyria. He settled them in Halah, in Gozan on the Habor River and in the towns of the Medes. All this took place because the Israelites had sinned against the LORD their God....'" says Bagautdin Kurbanov, a resident of the settlement of Khalag. "When

I read the Scriptures and saw this, I was astounded. Really, today also we are sinning against our Lord and Saviour. That is why we are a poor people."[28]

The passage quoted by this resident of Dagestan refers to the ancient Jewish people who were deported to the Caucasus region in 722 BC.[29] Perhaps Jewish settlement in Central Asia might originate from this event: certainly the 'Mountain Jews' of the Caucasus region have been living in the region for many centuries.[30] It is likely that the Jewish communities in Samarkand, Bukhara and Turkestan in southern Kazakstan date from Jewish settlers in the 7th—6th centuries BC. These settlers migrated there along with retreating Scythians (alternatively called Saks) who, in the first quarter of the seventh century BC, had invaded the Near East, going as far as Israel and Egypt, and for twenty-eight years had ruled Media, a country situated in the north-west of modern Iran.[31]

About one and a half thousand years later, in the 8th or early 9th century AD, many of the Khazar people living in the region between the Crimea and the north Caucasus adopted the Jewish faith. Initially Judaism was adopted by the Khazar leaders but many other Khazars followed their example. The Khazar language belonged to the Turkic linguistic group, so it was related to various modern languages of the region such as Kumyk, Nogai, Tatar, Azeri, Uzbek, Karakalpak, Kazak and so on. Between the 7th and 10th centuries AD the Khazar state was a significant power in a region between the Crimea and the Caspian Sea, including parts of the North Caucasus and some areas which are now in western Kazakstan and northwestern Uzbekistan.[32]

One of the outstanding features of the Khazar state was its tolerance of other religions: Muslims, Jews, Christians and pagans could all practise their religions freely without fear of persecution or harassment.[33] This was very unusual at that time and unfortunately such tolerance has also been rare in other states since then. Even atheists had the same kind of intolerance of other ideas during the twentieth century, when adherents of all religions suffered persecution in the USSR. To some extent the Communists feared the power of religion to influence people, and they also thought that religion was the 'opiate of the people'. However, I suspect that there were also moral issues at work. Officials who lied about production figures or bureaucrats who tried to project a false image of the glorious successes of Communism perhaps felt threatened by those who stood up for the values of honesty and truth. These values are rooted in the character of God himself. In the same way, those who believe that each human being is valuable because he or she was made by God and is loved by God might seem to be a threat to officials whose power rests on fear and exploitation. Truth (including honesty) and love (including compassion and kindness towards others) have to be the basis of any workable social group—whether it is a state, a business or a family. Those who try to live by these values are actually living more in the way that God himself intended them to live. However, we can best understand how to live this way if we know the God of Truth who is also the God of Love.

Both Islam and Christianity have their roots in Judaism and acknowledge the Jewish prophets as genuine spokesmen of the one true God. When God introduced himself to the prophet Musa, he said that he was the god of the ancestors of the Jewish people: "I am the God of your father, the God of Ibrahim, the God of Isaak and the God of Yakub."[34] The prophets Ibrahim, Isaak and Yakub were the ancestors of the Jewish people and nowadays they continue to be held in honour not only by Jews but also by Muslims and Christians. However, far more important than a respect for these prophets is a relationship with the one who introduced himself as the God of Ibrahim, Isaak and Yakub.

This God has been worshipped for many centuries by the ancestors of many peoples now living in Central Asia, although they might have worshipped this God using a variety of different forms of prayer, spoken in different languages and with various styles of worship. God is so great that he can understand prayers offered in Hebrew, Syriac, Arabic,

Chechen, Uzbek, Tajik and other languages—but what is far more important to God is the attitude of one's heart. God looks inside each one of us and sees the hidden motivations behind our prayers and our religious acts. He knows whether our religion is genuine or is merely an outward show.

God is the one who gives life to each of us in our mother's womb. He is also the one whom each of us will meet with after death. He is not only the source of our lives but also the destination of our lives. Our lives are a journey: that journey starts with God and also ends with God. However, each of us has a choice to make about whether or not we also invite God to be with us along the way as we make that journey.

This book is about a journey through Central Asia along parts of the Great Silk Road. It is also about the journey which each one of us makes with God. I have often travelled along various parts of the Great Silk Road and I love the people who live in these regions. I have a great respect for their cultures and way of life, and have learned so much from them about important values in life—such as hospitality, the way we should show respect for older people, the importance of family relationships, and so on. These are values which God also emphasises in the Holy Books through his prophets. Probably the peoples of Central Asia respect these values because their ancestors took seriously God's revelation through all his prophets over the centuries.

The Bible brings together in one volume the revelations given by God to various prophets at different times. We may think of the *Taurat*, *Zabur* and *Injil* as three separate books but they are all from God and that is why they are brought together in the Bible. In some ways I have done something a little similar in this book by bringing together in one volume some of my experiences which took place on a number of different visits to Central Asia. I have put them together in the form of a narrative which I have called a pilgrimage because life for all of us is a pilgrimage. We are all on a journey to God.

Along this journey I have often been helped by friends in Central Asia and the Caucasus. They have helped me not only in material ways, through hospitality and kindness, but, more importantly, the example of their lives has helped me on my pilgrimage. I have learned so much about generosity, for instance, through seeing the generous behaviour of my friends in Kyrgyzstan. I have learned about faith and trust in God through the example of a Kazak friend. My friends in Uzbekistan and Dagestan have shown me shining examples of what it means to persevere and not give up in the face of difficulties or hardships. These are lessons which we cannot learn from a book but we have to see them in real life to appreciate their meaning.

Some of my friends I have met at academic conferences but many of them I have just met 'along the way' while travelling in buses or planes, and so on. Sometimes I met them in Russia or other places and they invited me to visit them if I were to come to their country. It is this kind of warm-hearted and generous spirit which is so common throughout Central Asia and which is a great strength of these cultures.

My appreciation of my Central Asian friends also means that I want to respect their privacy too. That is why sometimes I have refrained from giving too many details about how or where we met, or about other personal details of their lives. Similarly, in writing about some of my friends, I have taken the liberty of changing their names or other circumstantial details so as to preserve their anonymity—even though some of them have given me permission to use their actual names. In the same way, the conversations recorded here are based on real ones but at times I have combined two or more dialogues together or have included some extra comments to explain a topic in more detail. For example, if I am talking with someone I might mention what a great prophet of God has said about a topic. However, it is better to be able to give the original quotation from the writings of that prophet. In such instances, I have here included the fuller quotation from the Holy Book and in a footnote have given the source of the quotation. I have taken these editorial liberties to make the essential topics of the discussions more easily understood. However, the deeper spiritual message is not changed at all. It is the deeper spiritual meaning which is important, as my friends in Central Asia easily recognise when they tell stories about a well-known person who is known in Kazak as *Kozhanasyr*, in Uighur as *Näsirdin Äfänti*, in Uzbek as *Nasriddin Afandi* (or just *Afandi*), in Turkish as *Nasrettin Hoca*, in Tajik as *Mushfiqi*—and so on in other languages.[35]

I mention him not just because he is known by a variety of

names but also because the stories about him can often be understood on different levels: "there is the joke, followed by a moral—and usually the little extra which brings the consciousness of the potential mystic a little further on the way to realization."[36] The same could be said of Aesop's fables or even of the parables told by Isa Mesih—that is, simple stories with deeper spiritual meanings.

My hope is that you, the reader, will also find here some new insights about deeper issues in life. You and I are both on a journey and we need to learn from one another about how to walk on the journey of life—but the best teacher of all is God himself.

I would like to dedicate this book to my friends in Central Asia and the Caucasus. Like you and me, they too are on a journey to God. My hope is that this book will help all of us to make that journey not only *to* God but also *with* God.

XINJIANG: ALMS

The hot Central Asian sun burned down from a cloudless blue sky as I got out of the bus at a small town in north-west China. I was heading westwards along the route of what used to be the Great Silk Road across Central Asia, linking China with Europe. My journey had started in the city of Xi'an, China, and was to take me through Kazakstan, Kyrgyzstan, Tajikistan, Uzbekistan, Turkmenistan, Azerbaijan and republics of the Caucasus included in the Russian Federation.

The bus driver had told us that the stop would last for half an hour, so I thought I had enough time to get something to eat. I noticed a vendor making and selling the flat, round bread which the Uighurs call '*naan*'—and which is known by a similar name in many other Central Asian languages. As I started to eat the one I had bought, I noticed an old Uighur man sitting begging, with a young boy next to him.

Perhaps it was merely curiosity, or perhaps it was a prompting from another source, but I felt that I wanted to find out more about this man. I decided to buy a second naan bread, which I then offered to the beggar. He looked up at me, surprise registering on his face—perhaps because I was not a local person—then said, "*Rekhmet*"—"Thank you".

"*Yakshı musız*" I said—a Uighur greeting which means, literally, "Are you all right?" It was one of a handful of Uighur expressions which I knew, so I was unable to carry on much of a conversation. I tried to ask him about himself in my limited Chinese but could not get very far apart from finding out that he was Uighur, had no job and that the child with him was his four-year old grandson.

Our limited conversation was interrupted by the bus driver calling me back onto the bus. Glancing out of the window, I saw the beggar waving goodbye to me. I waved back, wondering what kind of future lay ahead not only for him but more particularly for his grandson. Would he grow up thinking that all he needed to do in life was to sit by the roadside in order to get money? How much of an education would he receive? Would he be exploited by others, perhaps forced to beg too but to give some of what he received to those who manipulated him? Perhaps I would never know the answers.

My thoughts were suddenly interrupted by the man sitting next to me on the bus. His black hat with white embroidery indicated that he belonged to one of the local ethnic groups and he had already confirmed to me that he was Uighur. He was an intelligent man who had studied English at a university in Urumchi and my sitting next to him on the bus had given him an opportunity to practise his English.

"Why did you help that beggar?" he asked.

"Well, why not?" I replied—knowing, as I said it, that it was a rather weak reply. Basically, I was unsure why Ali had asked that question or how to answer it.

"In China, we might sometimes give a beggar some small change, but we don't usually stop to talk with them."

I was about to say something about each person being important, but then I changed my mind. Instead, I said, "I don't suppose beggars in China would ever give back money that they had just been given either."

"No, of course not!" replied Ali, "But not only in China—beggars in other countries wouldn't do that either."

2

"It happened to me once when I was passing through London—a beggar ran after me and gave me my money back!" I commented, quietly.

Beneath Ali's bushy eyebrows, his brown eyes widened.

"Why? Did you give him some fake money, or something?"

"No, not at all. It was real money and he was a real beggar."

"What did you do?" asked Ali. I could see that he really wanted to know so I began to tell him the story.

"The beggar was sitting in an underground passageway leading to a subway station. Nobody else was in the passageway as I approached. I knew that the beggar would ask me for money and I had to make a decision. Should I ignore the man and carry on, or should I stop and give him something?

Without spoken words, in my heart I prayed and asked God for wisdom. As I drew near to the beggar, the man looked at me and said, 'Can you help me?'

'What do you want?' I asked.

'Can you help me?' repeated the beggar.

'What do you want?' I said again.

'Can you spare some small change?' asked the beggar.

'What exactly do you want?' I replied.

'Have you enough for a cup of tea?' the beggar said.

'How much do you want?' I asked. The beggar hesitated a moment, then replied, 'Fifty pence'.

I reached my hand into my pocket and found fifty pence—that's something like five Yuan at the current exchange rate. Giving it to the man, I walked on towards the subway station.

Suddenly I was aware that the beggar was running after me. He caught up with me and gave me my money back.

'Here's your money', he said, 'Take it back. I don't want your money. What I really want is someone to talk with.'

I stopped, took back the money and I sat down with the beggar on the cold stone floor of the passageway. We talked with one another and I learned more about the man's life and why he was sitting there begging. For that beggar, the gift of my time and attention was far more valuable than the money."

Ali, who had been listening carefully to my story, was quiet for a short while, apparently thinking over what I had said. Finally, he asked,

"Why did you keep asking him again and again what he wanted?"

"I mentioned that at the beginning I had asked God for wisdom. I did not know what I should do, but when I prayed, into my mind came the story of a blind beggar who had called out to Isa Mesih, saying, 'Have mercy on me'.[37] It would have seemed to some of the bystanders that this beggar was asking Isa Mesih for money. They would not have understood Isa Mesih's reaction when he instead asked the beggar what he wanted. That blind man replied, 'Lord, let me see again'.[38] Isa Mesih then healed his eyes. This healing was a far more valuable gift than money."

"Yes, you are right," replied Ali, "There are many things money cannot buy. Money cannot buy genuine friendship or even sincere respect. It is like that Beatles song, 'Money can't buy me love'—and they were right. If we think that money brings us happiness then we are living under a delusion."

"That beggar whom I met in London recognised that he needed something more precious than money. However, most of us would prefer to give a few coins to a beggar and to hurry on rather than to stop and talk."

"We Uighurs do give money to beggars. Sometimes they come up to you when you leave a mosque because Muslims are supposed to give alms, what we call *zakat*."

"And do you help them?"

"Sometimes. I'd feel embarrassed going past them if I've just been in the mosque saying my prayers! So it's easier to give them something so that they don't pester you."

"Can I ask how much you give?"

"Oh, just a few coins—enough to stop them pestering me."

"And do you give other *zakat* to other people?"

"No, not really. Maybe if there is a disaster like an earth-quake and there are people in need I might give some money to a charity. But I admit that it's not as much as the imam says we should give—he says that *zakat* should be at least five percent of your income, or something like that. But I don't know anyone who would give away that much."

I decided not to tell him that the prophet Musa in the *Taurat* actually says that the Jews should give away ten per-cent of their income as a minimum, besides other freewill gifts above and beyond that. Many followers of Isa Mesih follow this same principle and regard ten percent of their income

5

as the minimum which they should give away. The *Injil* encourages generosity but does not specify a fixed percentage. Nevertheless, it seems to me that some people—whether they are Jews, Christians or Muslims—see the giving of alms as rather like a tax which they are obliged to give, but they do not recognise the more fundamental principles which are expressed through their giving.

"Let me tell you about a family I know in Kyrgyzstan," I said to Ali. "The wife, Bermet, is an educated woman who used to be a newspaper editor. Now she lives in a village where she looks after the family's cows while her husband works in Bishkek. Bermet does not have much income of her own, but she decided of her own volition that she would give away half of it for the work of God or to help those more needy than herself. Whenever she receives any money, she puts half of it into envelopes allocated for helping others. Then she can draw on the money to help people in need.

"Bermet has chosen to help others in this way because she feels that this is the amount which God has put on her heart as the right amount for her. She does not say that it is a law for everyone to give away half of their income to others. The principle is that of being generous to others, according to one's own circumstances."

Ali thought about this for a moment, then commented, "I've never heard of anyone who is so generous with their money like that. Of course, there are rich people who give a lot of their money away to charity, but they still have plenty for themselves. In reality they are not giving a very high proportion of their wealth. I think that real generosity is when a person gives sacrificially, like your friend Bermet."

"I agree with you—and, you know, God agrees with you too! God looks into the hearts of people who are giving money and God recognises what motivates them."

"But if God looks at the heart, why is he concerned about money and how much of it we give away?" queried Ali.

"Surely the gift of time and friendship is also a form of giving alms?" I commented to Ali. "That beggar in London who wanted someone to talk with him really had a greater need for words than for money. It is the same in our relationship with God: the prophet Musa said, 'Man does not live on bread alone but on every word that comes from the mouth of God.'[39] Isa Mesih also affirmed the same truth.[40] Many people are hungry in their spirits and need the word of God more than food or money."

"So you mean that they need to read a book? I thought it was interesting what you said how Isa Mesih quoted the words of the prophet Musa in the *Taurat*. It reminds me of what Allah said in the Qur'an, when he told the prophet, 'if you are in doubt as to what We have revealed to you, ask those who read the Book before you; certainly the truth has come to you from your Lord, therefore you should not be of the disputers.'[41] The Qur'an instructs us that we should also read the *Taurat*, *Zabur* and *Injil*."

"You are a wise man to know that great truth. However, when I was speaking with that beggar, even though I mentioned to him about what is written in God's written books, there was another book which he was reading and which was without words."

"What do you mean?"

7

"Written books are very important. However, people also read us like books: they see from our behaviour what is inside us. In the *Injil* it is written, 'You yourselves are our letter, written on our hearts, known and read by everyone'.[42] Whether or not we like to think of ourselves in this way, you and I are also 'books' and our actions show the content of what is inside us. It is therefore important that we show that the content of our hearts is good and is honouring to God—what God intends us to be."

Ali was silent for a moment, then commented, "So what is that to do with *zakat*?"

"Everything!" I replied. "People who think that they are discharging the religious duty of giving alms—*zakat*—when they give a token amount to a beggar outside a mosque or church are actually evading the real responsibilities which lie behind the principle of *zakat*. True *zakat* involves the responsibility to care for poor and needy people in every area of their lives, not only financially. It is a matter of the heart and of our attitudes inside, not just of what we do with our money."

"That's much too hard!" retorted Ali. "You can't expect people to spend all day chatting with each and every beggar they meet! It's far easier just to give them a bit of money and then get on with your life."

"I'm not saying that we have to stop and help each and every beggar. What I did with that one in London is not what I usually do—but it is what I felt God was telling me to do on that occasion. It is not like a 'magic formula'; it's not a law about what to do every time. Instead, it is a matter of listening to God. Let him show you his plan and what to do in a particular situation."

"And how do you do that? How does God speak to you?"

"It's not usually like audible words—although there was once when I did hear such words, which sounded like they were from outside me. I usually have a kind of deep conviction inside me, an inner voice, prompting me to do something, or bringing an idea to my mind."

"Are you talking about your conscience?"

"No, it's different to the voice of conscience—although I believe that often our conscience is also the voice of God speaking to us. What I'm talking about is more like a kind of intuition. However, that's not the only way God can speak to us; he may speak to us through dreams for example, but most important of all is the way that he speaks to us through the holy scriptures."

"For example?"

"Like when my wife and I felt God speaking to us about adopting children from orphanages. We already had three children of our own—two boys and a girl—and after the third child was born my wife felt that three was enough. So she was the one that God had to speak to, about ten years later, about taking on another child! My wife had learned about the many abandoned babies in China who were left on the streets or in parks—most of them baby girls, as their parents wanted to have a boy. It was then, while reading the *Taurat* and *Injil*, that she felt God speaking to her about his concern and love for orphans and others marginalized by society. It was as if those verses were being impressed on her heart as she read them. Ultimately it was a question of obedience—were we willing to do what we felt God was saying to us?"

"And you did?"

"It took about two years of bureaucracy and waiting for each of the two children we adopted, but at each step of the way we felt that God was opening the doors and providing for us."

"That's all right for Europeans, but here in China we can't afford to do such things."

"That's what a lot of people think—but it's not actually true. For example, when we adopted our first Chinese child, whose name in Chinese means 'Beautiful Fragrance', we also visited a village where we met a lady with three children; she told us that one of them had also been adopted from the orphanage where 'Beautiful Fragrance' had been living. Two years later, when we adopted 'Dawn Swallow', we were not allowed to look around inside the rooms of the orphanage where they looked after the children but we could at least see the outside of the building from the street. As we were standing there, a man came out of the orphanage gate and wondered what we were doing there. There was a whole group of us—not only my wife and myself but also our two teenage sons and our teenage daughter, plus our first adopted Chinese girl (who was then almost three years old) as well as our Chinese interpreter-guide and the driver of the mini-van. After the interpreter explained who we were, the man said something which made the interpreter's eyes open wide and her jaw drop in amazement."

"What did he say?" asked Ali.

"He said that he and his wife had four grown-up children of their own—born before the law on one birth per family was introduced—and then they adopted seventeen other children."

"Seventeen!" gasped Ali, "That's incredible... but why? Why should they do that?"

"That's exactly what we asked him too. He explained that he is a follower of Isa Mesih and that is why he and his wife want to show the love of God to others."

"Which was why you had adopted those two Chinese children too?"

"Yes. When we told this man, Dr. Zhu, that it was also our motivation in adopting them, his face beamed and he said in Chinese, '*Feichang hao, feichang hao*—excellent, excellent".[43]

"So do you think we should all go around adopting children from orphanages?" asked Ali.

"Each one of us has something we can do," I replied. "As I said before, it is a question of finding God's plan for each one of us and listening to his guidance. It is not a matter of rules, which is the problem with those who think of *zakat* as a kind of tax and think that if they have given away a certain percentage of their income then they have paid their tax to God and fulfilled their duty. However, God is much more concerned with the attitude of our hearts than with the amount of money we give away or whatever other kind deeds we do. We cannot buy our way into heaven. That is why our giving to others has to be voluntary, from the heart. It should be an expression of love, not as a duty or a kind of 'tax'. Nevertheless, when we do give from the heart, we should do so generously. In the holy book it is written:

> Each one of you should give just as he has decided in his heart, not reluctantly or under compulsion, because God loves a cheerful giver.[44]"

11

"A cheerful giver? I don't know many people who are cheerful about giving away money!"

"It is a question of the heart, of our attitude: do we give grudgingly or generously? I suppose an example of this is shown too by an incident in the life of Isa Mesih." I paused and found the place in the *Injil* where it is written that Isa Mesih

> sat down opposite the offering box, and watched the crowd putting coins into it. Many rich people were throwing in large amounts. And a poor widow came and put in two small copper coins, worth less than a penny. He called his disciples and said to them, "I tell you the truth, this poor widow has put more into the offering box than all the others. For they all gave out of their wealth. But she, out of her poverty, put in what she had to live on, everything she had."[45]

Then I added, "This is a principle for us too."

"What? You mean we too are supposed to give away everything we have to live on, like you say that widow did?" interjected Ali.

"God wants us to be prepared to give generously, no matter what our income," I replied. "He deserves the very best that we can give, not only in terms of money but also through giving love, care and time to others. Giving money is the 'easy way' to give alms, but Dr. Zhu and his wife show the kind of sacrifice that is real *zakat*. Every day they have great demands not only on their money but also on their time and energy as they show love to children who had suffered the pain of being rejected by their own parents and sometimes of being left in the street to die."

"But we can't all be like that, or like Mother Theresa in India—who received the Nobel Peace Prize for her work of compassion among poor people," remarked Ali.

"Someone once told me a quotation from her which says that an ocean is made up of many drops. What she was saying was that each one of us can do our little bit, even though it might seem like a drop in the ocean—or, as they say in Chinese, like a grain of millet in a granary.[46] We may not be able to adopt seventeen children like Dr. Zhu, but we can each do our small part. In the *Injil* it is written: 'Religion that God our Father accepts as pure and faultless is this: to look after orphans and widows in their distress and to keep oneself from being polluted by the world.'"[47]

"Yes, here in China there are many needy people," admitted Ali, "and not only in China but also in other countries too. For example, in Laos I have seen children malnourished and poorly clothed because their parents were addicted to opium and spent most of their money on that drug."

"How did you feel when you saw them?"

"I felt sorry for them. They were dirty and poorly dressed, some without shoes. I felt that I wanted to help them but I did not know how."

"You are a compassionate man, Ali. Do you know that in feeling that kind of compassion you were actually feeling a little of what is in God's heart?"

"Really? I had heard that God is compassionate—but does he really care for those kinds of children? I always thought he was rather distant and aloof."

"If you feel love and compassion for those who are suffering, where do you think those feelings come from? In this,

13

you are reflecting the nature of God himself, who is compassionate and loving towards those he has made."

"I'd never thought of it that way before," commented Ali.

"In fact, *zakat* reflects the nature of God even more deeply than this. God gives more generously than any of us. God is far more generous than Dr. Zhu in China or Mother Theresa in India. God also lives up to his own principles. Like any good leader, God does not expect of others what he is not prepared to do himself. He will not demand of us what he himself is not willing to do."

"Surely you don't mean that God himself pays *zakat*?"

"In a way, yes, I do mean that."

"But how could God himself possibly pay *zakat*?"

"As I said, God also lives up to his own principles. Think of any kind of sacrifice which God asks us to make, and you will find that God himself is prepared to do the same, or even more."

Ali thought for a while, then said, "But what about the time when God himself asked the prophet Ibrahim to give his own son as a sacrifice? We remember this event every year when we sacrifice a ram and share its meat with others. This festival reminds us of the prophet Ibrahim's willingness to sacrifice even the son whom God had given to him in fulfilment of God's promise. The prophet Ibrahim had already bound up his own son and had laid him out as a sacrifice. He had even taken the knife and was about to plunge it into the heart of his own son when God spoke to him through an angel and said, 'Ibrahim! Ibrahim!... Do not lay a hand on the boy.... Do not do anything to him. Now I know that you fear God, because you have not withheld from me your son, your only son.'[48] Ibrahim then looked up and saw a ram caught by its horns in a thicket, which he sacrificed instead of his son. So, if God was demanding that the prophet Ibrahim give up his son as a sacrifice—even though in the end God did stop him doing this—are you saying that God himself would be willing to do the same as he asked the prophet Ibrahim to do? Surely not!"

"That is exactly my point: God is too great to demand anything of mankind which he himself would not do. How do we know this? Think about the prophet Yahya [John the Baptist], who lived centuries after the time of the prophet Ibrahim. One day the prophet Yahya saw someone coming towards him and announced, 'Look, the Lamb of God who takes away the sin of the world!'[49] Do you know whom the prophet Yahya saw?"

"I don't know, who was it that the prophet saw? Who could possibly be the one who takes away the sin of the world?"

"It was Isa Mesih."

"What a strange comment to make!" interposed Ali, "Why did the prophet Yahya describe Isa Mesih as 'the Lamb of God who takes away the sin of the world'?"

"The prophet Yahya knew about the ram which was killed by the prophet Ibrahim so that his own son could live. However, God was doing something far greater than sending a ram to die instead of just one person. He was sending a far better sacrifice who was willing to die instead of each one of us. Only a human being can really take the place of another human being. Only a person without sin could die as a sacrifice for those who are dirty and imperfect and full of sin. That one was Isa Mesih."

15

"How could Isa Mesih be without sin? Surely everyone sins?" commented Ali.

"He was the only one who was perfect. Those who lived closely with him for about three years afterwards wrote that Isa Mesih 'committed no sin' and 'in him there is no sin'.[50] You could not be with me for even three days and say that about me! Isa Mesih himself challenged his enemies, saying 'Who among you can prove me guilty of any sin?'—but they could not answer him.[51] However, there is a very deep reason why Isa Mesih was without sin. Can you imagine what that might be?"

Ali thought for a moment, then said, "Tell me".

"Do you know how close Isa Mesih was to God?"

"No. How close?"

"Isa Mesih is described both in the *Injil* and also in the Qur'an as the 'Word of God'.[52] Do you know what this means?

"No, tell me."

"This is what the *Injil* says about the Word of God," I replied, then read the words:

> In the beginning was the Word, and the Word was with God, and the Word was God. He was with God in the beginning. Through him all things were made; without him nothing was made that has been made. In him was life, and that life was the light of men...[53]

"But Isa Mesih was a person, not a Word!"

"Later it says: 'The Word became flesh and lived for a while among us.'[54] This refers to the time when Isa Mesih left heaven to live in this world. However, the same passage

16

also describes how people rejected the Word of God—Isa Mesih—when he came to live among us. It is written:

> He was in the world, and though the world was made through him, the world did not recognise him. He came to that which was his own, but his own did not receive him. Yet to all who received him, to those who believed in his name, he gave the right to become children of God—children born not of natural descent, nor of human decision or a husband's will, but born of God.[55]

"But surely God is too great to have a child! You do not mean that he had sex with a human woman, do you?"

"No. The passage says that these children are not born in the normal way. I think of it rather like our adopted Chinese children. They are not genetically my offspring but they are really our children in all other ways. They have the same relationship with us as our own natural children have. That is what it means to have a new relationship with God which is so close that we can say it is like that between a parent and child."

"I had never thought before that I could become like an adopted child of God."

"Yes, you can have that kind of a relationship with God. At first our own adopted children did not know all the time and effort, not to mention cost, which went into the process of our adopting them. We can say that we are like the Chinese orphans adopted by Dr. Zhu. However, God himself also gives sacrificially so that we too can be adopted into his family. God's self-sacrificial love is such that he sent the one nearest to his heart into the world, knowing that some would reject him. However, God's purpose was that all those who would receive Isa Mesih could be adopted into the family of God. It is written in the *Injil*: 'If God is for us, who can be against us? Indeed, he who did not spare his own Son, but gave him up for us all—how will he not also, along with him, freely give us all things?"[56] This is God's *zakat*."

XINJIANG: FASTING

The road seemed to be a thin line across the landscape, separating the mountains to our right from the desert to our left. For many centuries people have taken this route on their way into or out of China. I reflected on the significance of the route as the main Western doorway of China. The deserts and mountains have been a barrier to many, but also a challenge to those willing to take the risks. They had different motives: some wanted knowledge—even if it was merely out of curiosity—whereas others wanted to find wealth—or at least goods for trading. Some may have been looking for freedom in a new and unknown land. Whatever their motivations, they embarked on a journey which led on a thin trail between danger and opportunity.

Some lines across the landscape are made by God, others are man-made. The thin line we were travelling on was one which connects: it joins up oases but also connects China with Central Asia—and, ultimately, with Europe. For a long time the natural barriers of deserts, mountains and steppe had helped to isolate China from the rest of Eurasia—but it was a permeable barrier. To reinforce it, the Chinese drew another line across the landscape between the deserts of north-west China and the Pacific ocean. Although it connected up earlier defensive walls, the purpose of the Great Wall was to mark a line of division: steppe versus cultivated land, nomad versus farmer, Mongolians versus Chinese.

I glanced across at Ali, who was watching the film being shown on the television at the front of the bus. Although he was ethnically Uighur, he was probably, like all of us, carrying genes from many different types of peoples. At the museum in Urumchi I had been looking at the remains of a person who might have been one of Ali's ancestors. Three thousand years ago she was buried in the desert of Xinjiang. Now her body is one of several on display at the museum of history in Urumchi. Who was she? What did she think about life in Central Asia? Her hopes, her fears, what she loved and what she hated are unknown; we can only speculate by looking at what archaeologists found associated with her.

She is known to us only because her body was well preserved in the very arid conditions of Xinjiang. However, the features of these ancient Central Asian people in some ways resembled Europeans—testimony to the high degree of inter-cultural and inter-ethnic contact over the millennia in this part of the world.

I was reminded of what my Russian friends had said: "Scratch a Russian and you will find a Tatar." What were the genetic origins of my two adopted Chinese children? We do not know. However, most people around the world, not only in Central Asia but also in Russia, China and other continents, have ancestors from many different ethnic groups. V. I. Lenin, for example, is reported to have had an Asiatic grandmother, whose ethnicity was Kalmyk.[57] In Afghanistan, people with blue eyes are thought to have ancestors among the Greek soldiers who entered the area at the time of Alexander the Great. Likewise, descendants of Mongolian troops can be found throughout the former Mongolian empire, including the Hazara people of Afghanistan and Mongolian residents of Xinmeng township in the Tonghai county of Yunnan province, in the south-west of China.[58] In Central Asia today probably most people have genes from ancestors belonging to many different ethnic groups, such as Sogdians, Bactrians, Persians, Turks, Chinese, Mongolians and others.

In fact, almost all populations in the world have had some mixture over the centuries with other peoples: that very fact in itself—the fact that we can interbreed, can mix up our genes—shows that we all belong to one species and that the divisions we try to construct between one another are rather artificial. Ultimately, we are all descendants of the first human beings, all one family.

Next to me, Ali shifted in his seat. The credits were rolling up the screen but nobody was interested in knowing the names of those who had acted the minor parts. Most of us play minor parts in the great drama of life and our names are forgotten later. As the wise prophet Suleiman commented, 'There is no remembrance of men of old, and even those who are yet to come will not be remembered by those who follow.'[59] Suleiman was a king who had the opportunity to try to find meaning to life through wealth, through knowledge, through pleasure, and in other ways too, but in the end he realised that none of these bring fulfilment; none of them is what life is really about.

Suleiman referred to created things as being 'under the sun' but none of them has meaning in itself without reference to the one who is beyond the sun—that is, God. In the end, Suleiman realised that life without God is meaningless. God created each of us for a reason—and our lives only find true meaning when we discover that purpose.

Ali reached into his bag, pulled out a couple of apples and offered one to me.

"*Rekhmet*," I said, taking one of them.

"Are you allowed to eat the forbidden fruit?" joked Ali.

"You mean apples? Actually, the *Taurat*, the Holy Book of the prophet Musa, doesn't tell us what kind of fruit was on the tree of the knowledge of good and evil. I know that pictures usually show it as an apple but that was only because in Latin the name for apple—'*malum*'—sounded like the word for bad, '*malus*'. Personally, I wouldn't be surprised if the forbidden fruit was actually a bunch of juicy grapes!"

"Why do you say that? Because we have such wonderful grapes here in Xinjiang?"

"No—I said it just because taking one little grape out of a big bunch is not as noticeable or obvious as taking a bite out of an apple! A lot of us start to sin like that—because we think of it as something small which wouldn't make any difference."

"Hmm... like my first cigarette!" remarked Ali.

"Probably—and now what's the result of that?"

"Twenty a day—and I can't stop!"

"Well, at least you're honest about it!" I said, with a smile.

A little later, when Ali lit up another cigarette, I decided to revert to the topic and asked him, "Would you like to give up smoking if you could?"

He thought about it for a little while, then replied, "I'm not sure. On the one hand, it is a bad habit and I know it's bad for my health, but I really can't imagine life without cigarettes. I seem to need them."

"Yes," I replied. "In some ways I also have that problem with chocolate!"

Ali seemed relieved. He smiled and said, "I was afraid you were going to push me like you pushed that beggar, asking me what I really want!"

"I did wonder about that—just like Isa Mesih asked a man who had been crippled for thirty-eight years, 'Do you want to get well?'[60] In your case, however, you obviously already know the answer yourself!"

"Anyway, there's nothing about smoking in the Qur'an or even in the Bible! That's what I tell people who say that I shouldn't smoke during Ramadan!"

"So you observe the Fast?" I probed.

"As far as I can, but it's hard. It's very difficult here in China. When I was a student, it was even more difficult."

"In what way?"

"I remember the time when a fellow student came up to me and said, 'Would you like to join me for lunch?' It was a simple question but I was put on the spot. I said, 'Sorry, I'm not feeling well today and I don't feel like eating' but afterwards I felt guilty about it, knowing that I had told a lie. 'Which is the greater sin,' I wondered, 'to tell a lie or not to observe the fast?' Even though I had eaten very early that morning, I was really hungry but I was afraid to admit that I was fasting."

"So why didn't you want to admit to it?" I asked, already suspecting the answer.

"I knew that here in China some students had been expelled from the school for practising their religion. It is difficult, as you are expected to behave like a good Communist but all our relatives say you have to be a good Muslim too."

23

"I can understand a little of that dilemma, though for a different reason. For me, it is difficult when I am visiting people and they invite me to eat with them but I am fasting. I don't want to tell them that I am fasting, because Isa Mesih said that when we fast it we should do it without making it obvious to others."

"I didn't know that! Why did he say that?"

"Because people in his day wanted to show off to others how religious they were! So Isa Mesih said, 'When you fast, do not look sullen like the hypocrites, for they make their faces unattractive so that people will see them fasting. I tell you the truth, they have their reward. When you fast, put oil on your head and wash your face, so that it will not be obvious to others when you are fasting, but only to your Father who is in secret. And your Father, who sees in secret, will reward you.'[61]"

"So you do fast then?"

"Sometimes, especially when there is something special I want to pray for."

"Such as?"

"When there is something really on my heart that I am concerned about. I suppose the best examples are the times when I fasted and prayed specially for one or the other of my children when they were teenagers and going through difficult periods."

"How long did you fast for?"

"Twice I fasted for ten days, but usually it is less than that—maybe a few days or so."

"But you ate at night, like we do, I suppose?"

"No, just drank water."

"For ten days! But I thought that when followers of Isa Mesih fast, they don't really fast—they just give up eating meat or some foods."

"There are some people who do that, but there are others who fast much more than I do—perhaps for a few weeks with nothing but water or juice."

"So why do you go without food altogether? Surely God created food and gives it to us as something good? He designed us that way, so we should eat and drink. So why should he tell us not to have it?"

"That's a very good question. One of the reasons is the example of Isa Mesih himself, who fasted for a period of forty days in the desert."

"That's almost six weeks! Do you mean he went without any food at all?"

"The *Injil* says, 'He ate nothing during those days, and when they were completed, he was famished'.[62] I don't know what he did about drinking."

"He must have been starving! So I suppose he then had a big feast to make up for it, like we do in the evenings during Ramadan?"

"Actually, he was tempted by the devil to use his spiritual authority and power to satisfy his hunger by miraculously turning stones into bread. However, he resisted this and other temptations by quoting from the *Taurat*. In this case, Isa Mesih replied to the devil, 'It is written: "Man does not live on bread alone, but on every word that comes from the mouth of God".[63] That's a good example for us too, when faced with temptation: it helps if we know what God has already said in the Holy Books."

"You mentioned previously that verse about living on every word that comes from the mouth of God. However, whenever I have experienced temptations and opposition from the evil one I had never thought before now about quoting the *Taurat* to the devil! Maybe I should try doing that. But I don't suppose it will take away my feelings of hunger and thirst when I am observing the Fast—or my craving for a cigarette!"

"Maybe you should try it and see what happens! But why do you observe the Fast anyway? What is your motivation for doing it?"

"Partly, I suppose it's because a lot of other people are doing it and I don't want to be different. But also I do it because God has commanded us to do so."

"So you sincerely want to do God's will?"

"As best I can, yes."

"Do you know what the prophet Isaiah says about what real fasting involves?"

"No. Who was the prophet Isaiah?"

"Isaiah was a prophet of God who lived about 700 years before Isa Mesih. At that time, like today, many people were fasting for the wrong reasons and motives. They saw fasting as a religious duty to be performed at certain times. However, they were not observing God's other commands to care for other people and to treat other people fairly, without cheat-

ing them. God spoke through the prophet Isaiah to explain
the real meaning of fasting." I opened my Bible and read the
following words:

'Why have we fasted,' they say,
'and you have not seen it?
Why have we humbled ourselves,
and you have not noticed?'
"Yet on the day of your fasting, you do as you please
and exploit all your workers.

Your fasting ends in quarreling and strife,
and in striking each other with wicked fists.
You cannot fast as you do today
and expect your voice to be heard on high.

Is this the kind of fast I have chosen,
only a day for a man to humble himself?
Is it only for bowing one's head like a reed
and for lying on sackcloth and ashes?
Is that what you call a fast,
a day acceptable to the LORD ?

"Is not this the kind of fasting I have chosen:
to loose the chains of injustice
and untie the cords of the yoke,
to set the oppressed free
and break every yoke?

Is it not to share your food with the hungry
and to provide the poor wanderer with shelter—
when you see the naked, to clothe him,
and not to turn away from your own flesh and blood?[64]

"For the prophet Isaiah, true fasting was not a matter of
the outward observance of a ritual but rather was an expression of the person's relationship with God. That relationship
is also expressed in the way we treat other people. To stop
eating so as to observe a religious duty is meaningless if at the

same time we are quarrelling and fighting among ourselves and not helping the poor and oppressed. What would Isaiah say today about those who seem to be religious people, who observe the prescribed times for fasting but who also take bribes and pervert the course of true justice?"

"Very true!" replied Ali. "Some people around here need to learn about the prophet Isaiah!"

"The prophet Isaiah said that fasting is meaningless if we do not care for our fellow human beings," I continued. "This is very similar to the teaching of Isa Mesih when he was asked which is the greatest commandment. He replied, "'Love the Lord your God with all your heart and with all your soul and with all your mind." This is the first and greatest commandment. And the second is like it: "Love your neighbour as yourself." All the Law and the Prophets hang on these two commandments.'[65] So fasting is not an end in itself but rather a means to an end—to help us to get to know God better."

"But I still don't understand why we should give up food that God created us to eat."

"Perhaps we can have some insight into the nature of fasting if we think of the times when we naturally do not want to eat. Very often people who are bereaved and are mourning naturally fast because they lose their appetite. In such circumstances fasting expresses their feelings of grief. In the same way, fasting can be an expression of our grief at our sin and of our wanting to repent of it. If we think of fasting as a form of grieving, we can understand why it can be an aid to sincere prayer of repentance."

"But what if I don't have such sins that I should grieve over? If Isa Mesih had no sin, he surely was not grieving over his own sins or repenting when he fasted."

"You are right in saying that Isa Mesih had no sin. In fact, he was the only one with no sin—but I think that when he fasted he was probably entering into another type of grieving which is greater than that of grieving over our own sins. It is the grief of a parent who weeps and grieves for a disobedient child. The parent loves the child so much that he or she is grieved to see the way that the child persistently makes the wrong choices in life. Our fasting can sometimes take this form of grieving too."

"Do you mean that God also feels towards us like a parent feels towards a child?"

"God is so much greater than we can understand, but if we can feel that kind of emotion because God made us that way, then God can share in such feelings too. For example, imagine the grief of the parents of a sixteen year old boy in Dagestan—that is, in the Caucasus region of the Russian Federation—who ran away from home and got involved with a group of friends in St. Petersburg who were taking narcotics. Before long he became addicted to drugs and, to finance his addiction, began to steal. Twice he was put in prison but he again returned to his old way of life, taking drugs and stealing again. Then his health deteriorated, with liver and kidney problems. His legs gave way and he could not walk. For two weeks he lay, without food, on some pipes in the roof of a building. There he began to pray, 'God, if you exist, help me'.

At that time God moved the hearts of some godly people who felt that God was telling them to go up to that roof, where they discovered this man. They took him to their drug rehabilitation centre where in time he was set free from his addictions—not by medicines or the help of doctors but through the prayers and love of the people of God. His health was restored and he got a job and began to live a normal life. In all that time he had never returned to his parents in Makhachkala, Dagestan, but after all these changes in his life he felt that God wanted him to go back and be reconciled with his parents. Can you imagine how they felt to see again their long-lost son?"

"How do you know this? Have you met these people?"

"It was the son himself who told me this story when I was in Dagestan. However, God feels that same way about us. We are like long-lost wayward children but God is waiting for us to come back to him and to discover the joy of a restored relationship."

"How do we do that? How can our relationship with God be restored?"

"Let me tell you about another son. This is a story which Isa Mesih told, to illustrate the feelings that God has when we, his long-lost wayward children, come back to him in true repentance:

> There was a man who had two sons. The younger one said to his father, "Father, give me my share of the estate." So he divided his property between them.

> Not long after that, the younger son got together all he had, set off for a distant country and there squandered his wealth in wild living. After he had spent everything, there was a severe famine in that whole country, and he began to be in need. So he went and hired himself out to a citizen of that country, who sent him to his fields to feed pigs. He longed to fill his stomach with the pods that the pigs were eating, but no-one gave him anything.

> When he came to his senses, he said, "How many of my father's hired men have food to spare, and here I am starving to death! I will set out and go back to my father

and say to him: Father I have sinned against heaven and against you. I am no longer worthy to be called your son; make me like one of your hired men." So he got up and went to his father.

But while he was still a long way off, his father saw him and was filled with compassion for him; he ran to his son, threw his arms around him and kissed him.

The son said to him, "Father I have sinned against heaven and against you. I am no longer worthy to be called your son."

But the father said to his servants, "Quick! Bring the best robe and put it on him. Put a ring on his finger and sandals on his feet. Bring the fattened calf and kill it. Let's have a feast and celebrate. For this son of mine was dead and is alive again; he was lost and is found." So they began to celebrate.

Meanwhile, the older son was in the field. When he came near the house, he heard music and dancing. So he called one of the servants and asked him what was going on. "Your brother has come," he replied, "and your father has killed the fattened calf because he has him back safe and sound."

The older brother became angry and refused to go in. So his father went out and pleaded with him. But he answered his father, "Look! All these years I've been slaving for you and never disobeyed your orders. Yet you never gave me even a young goat so I could celebrate with my friends. But when this son of yours who has squandered your property with prostitutes comes home, you kill the fattened calf for him!"

"My son," the father said, "you are always with me, and everything I have is yours. But we had to celebrate and be glad, because this brother of yours was dead and is alive again; he was lost and is found."[66]

I stopped reading from the *Injil*. Ali looked at me and said, "Carry on."

"That's the end of the story", I replied.

"But why does it stop there? What happened next?"

"What do you think? Isa Mesih told this story because he was being criticised by the religious leaders who thought that he was keeping company with the 'wrong sort' of people."

"Like your sitting with a beggar on the street?"

"Maybe something like that, but Isa Mesih was associating with those who were known to be engaged in sin of various kinds. He told this story because the attitude of the older brother in the story is like that of many religious people who do everything they think God wants, including fasting at the prescribed times. However, they do not understand the extent to which God grieves for those who are lost."

"I had never thought that God can grieve."

"Yes, God does grieve. The *Taurat* says:

The LORD saw how great man's wickedness on the earth had become, and that every inclination of the thoughts of his heart was only evil all the time. The LORD was grieved that he had made man on the earth, and his heart was filled with pain.[67]

"God—feel pain? Can God feel pain? That seems too much to accept!" interjected Ali.

32

"But that is what the *Taurat* says! This is the Holy Book which the prophet Musa compiled. God grieves and feels pain because of our sin and wrongdoing."

"In that case, think how much God must be grieving over the sins of the whole world," remarked Ali.

"Certainly. Just as parents want to have a close and loving relationship with their own children, God also created human beings so that we could know him in a special way.

"When we fast, we too have discomfort and hunger pains. In this way, fasting is a way in which we can also share in the pain of God. If we are fasting on behalf of someone else, grieving over that person's sin while we are praying for them, we are experiencing in a small way the kind of pain which God feels in his heart as he grieves over the sin and waywardness of the human race."

Ali thought about this for a moment, then asked, "And is that the only meaning of fasting?"

"No, there is even more to it," I replied, "because fasting is also a time when we recognise that spiritual values are far more important than earthly, material things—namely, food and drink. Food and drink are important and God-given parts of our lives. However, when we fast, we voluntarily give up something which is good for the sake of that which is even better. In this process, we also experience pain but we do it voluntarily for the sake of bringing benefit to others."

"But how can our pain benefit other people?" asked Ali, "That doesn't make sense to me."

"In everything there is a cost. If we want something, we have to work for it—or, you might say, we suffer so that we can get something better. For example, a mother giving birth suffers not for her own sake but for the sake of the child. This illustrates an important spiritual principle about sacrificing something good for the sake of that which is even better. In this way, fasting expresses something close to the heart of God. In the *Injil* it is written:

> Do nothing out of selfish ambition or vain conceit, but in humility consider others better than yourselves. Each of you should look not only to your own interests, but also to the interests of others.

> Your attitude should be the same as that of Isa Mesih: who, being in very nature God,
> did not consider equality with God something to be grasped,
> but made himself nothing,
> taking the very nature of a servant,
> being made in human likeness.
> and being found in appearance as a man,
> he humbled himself
> and became obedient to death –
> even death on a cross![68]

In this way, Isa Mesih did something which embodies the very spirit of fasting. He voluntarily left heaven in order to come to earth and become a human being. Even then he continued to suffer, even to the extent of being put to death on a cross. However, he did this for our sakes, so that we may have an opportunity to receive eternal life in heaven. Isa Mesih gave up that which was good—his life with God in heaven—in order to share the opportunity of life in heaven with us."

"So you are saying that fasting is a voluntary giving up of something good and God-given, for the sake of something which is better?"

"Yes—and Isa Mesih suffered far more than we do when we fast. It was as if the whole of his life was lived in the spirit of humility and self-denial which is the essence of fasting. In dying on our behalf, Isa Mesih suffered voluntarily for the sake of others. He gave up what is good for the sake of that which is best—namely, the salvation of our souls. In this, Isa Mesih demonstrates the true meaning of fasting.

However, it did not end with death on the cross! God raised Isa Mesih to life again and exalted him to the highest place, at the right hand of God in heaven. Now he invites us to join him in a celebration in heaven. It is like the celebration in the story quoted earlier about the wayward son. They celebrated the restored relationship. If we understand the real meaning of fasting as a turning from our sins and denying our own selves, we too can join with Isa Mesih to share in God's celebration in heaven."

KAZAKSTAN: WHEN GOD SPEAKS

Although the Tian Shan mountains mark a geographical and political border, it seemed to me that the cultural border is not so distinct. Certainly there is the change from the Arabic and Chinese writing to a Cyrillic script, and the previous Russian influence in Almaty does make it feel somewhat more 'European'. Nevertheless, I feel that among the Uighurs, Kazaks, Kyrgyz and other Central Asian peoples the Tian Shan marks a difference more like that between red and pink than that between red and blue.

Ali had not travelled with me as far as the border because he was travelling only as far as Yining, in the Ili valley. I had travelled on alone on a different bus going into Kazakstan. Arriving in Almaty, I again marvelled at the amount of greenery in the city, with tree-lined avenues in abundance providing plenty of shade from the intense sunlight. The city seems to change every time I visit and is now like a butterfly compared with the 'chrysalis' stage when I first saw it in 1990.

I had been back to Almaty several times since then and had made friends with quite a few Kazaks, Uighurs and others living in the city. At times I had attended academic conferences and other events at which issues of religion and culture were discussed. Such meetings provided opportunities to meet representatives of various different religions—including Muslims, Christians and even Hindus. One of the people I had met was a Muslim leader who was the Dean of an Islamic

Institute. Out of respect for his privacy, I shall call him by the pseudonym "Shamil" instead of his actual name.

Having returned to Almaty, I was interested in meeting up again with Shamil. My motivation was simply to keep up the contact which we already had and to get to know him better as a friend. I found his phone number and called him.

"Hello, is Shamil there?" I asked, in Russian.

"This is Shamil. Who is speaking?"

"This is David. Do you remember how we met at that conference in 2001?"

"David? Oh yes, David! You're one of those people who do not pray to icons or to the Virgin Mary! Nice to hear from you again."

I was not expecting this kind of description of myself! Momentarily, I recalled his comment at the conference, when, in a discussion with two Kazak pastors, he remarked that they had more things in common than he had thought. Previously I had overheard Shamil saying to another man that people should not pray to icons or to the Virgin Mary because it is like idolatry. He was amazed to discover that these followers of Isa Mesih agreed with him—and that they do not do such things either. Shamil had come to understand and respect the faith of these people who want a direct and simple relationship with God and who also love Isa Mesih.

"I'm back in Almaty again," I continued. "Is there any chance of meeting up?"

"Yes, of course! It would be a pleasure! Where are you staying?"

I gave him the details and we arranged to meet. Shamil's brother came to meet me too and we together went to their home, where I was treated to their generous hospitality. His wife told me that she was Ingush, from the North Caucasus. I assumed that she was descended from those who had been deported from the North Caucasus to Central Asia by order of Stalin.

After we had talked about many other things, Shamil's brother suddenly brought up the question of religion. I agreed with him that there is only one God and that we should worship him alone. However, the brother then began to insist that I should say the words, "There is no god but Allah"—and to say it in Arabic.

"But I do not speak Arabic," I said.

"That doesn't matter. Just repeat the syllables after me..."

"But if I do not understand the language, and it makes no sense to me, I cannot sincerely say the words from the heart. God understands all languages, not just Arabic, and to speak with God we have to speak sincerely. It is not a magic formula!"

At this point, Shamil intervened.

"I'm sorry," he said, "We were treating you like a village peasant! Of course, you are right: the words have to be sincere and from the heart. I am sorry that my brother was rather enthusiastic!"

Later that evening Shamil and his brother escorted me back to where I was staying and we parted amicably. I was glad that we had been able to meet up again. However, I felt that we had talked so much about ideas and doctrines that there had been no opportunity to ask him about his own experience of the power of God. Of course, it is important to believe the right things *about* God but it is vital that we also have a personal experience of God's presence and power working in our lives.

Some people like to discuss at great length ideas about God and the discussions seem to go round and round in circles! It might be to some extent a problem of finding the right words. Our human languages reflect human experience but how can we talk about heavenly or spiritual matters in words based on our experience in this world? God is so much greater than we can understand or express in words. When words fail, we might try to express our feelings about God through music or art but even these are poor reflections of a reality that we cannot convey in human expressions.

Rather than discussing at length about the nature of God, sometimes we simply need to ask God himself to show us his truth or power. For example, once when I was in Kazan, a Tatar man named Kurbangali came up to ask me a question. He wanted to know the truth about the right way to get to know God. Kurbangali had been reading the *Injil* but was unsure whether or not he should follow Isa Mesih.

In this situation, I felt that Kurbangali did not need to hear more words from a human being. Instead, I offered to pray with him and to ask God to show him the realities of his spiritual condition. Kurbangali was silent while I prayed to God and invited God's Holy Spirit to come onto Kurbangali and to reveal the truth to him.

Suddenly, Kurbangali looked up at me and said, "You're hypnotising me!"

"No, I'm not," I replied. "But why do you say that?"

"While you were praying, I became aware of a horrible black thing on my shoulder which suddenly lifted off me and went."

"I'm not hypnotising you," I said, "because I never suggested to you that anything like that might happen to you. However, there was an evil spirit on you which you became aware of, but it had to go when I invited God's Holy Spirit to come."

"Oh!" said Kurbangali, thoughtfully.

"Moreover," I continued, "This was a sign from God of his power. It was not your imagination because I know of other people who have experienced the same kind of thing when I've prayed with them for a demon to leave them."

I then told Kurbangali about a Russian woman who told me that she often had nightmares. When I asked her when they had first started, she told me it was after she had watched on television an occultist named Vladimir Kashpirovsky. In these circumstances, it was obvious that it was an evil spirit which was causing her nightmares, so in the name and authority of Isa Mesih I commanded the evil spirit to leave her. She too felt something oppressive lift off her. Some time later she told me that from then on the nightmares had stopped.

Not all disturbing dreams necessarily come from demons. Sometimes they might be from a troubled conscience. This was probably the case with a Tatar man named Ilgiz who once asked me to pray against his bad dreams. We prayed together and he asked God to forgive his sins. Ilgiz also invited Isa Mesih to become his Saviour and the Lord of his life. From that time on, his sleep became much sounder and untroubled.

Some dreams, however, clearly come from God. Often they are in story form and we have to think about their hidden meanings. In the same way, Isa Mesih often told stories about ordinary events but they carried a deeper spiritual message. Usually, however, his listeners had to think about the stories and work out the inner message.

Often God is speaking to us in our dreams about our spiritual condition. He may be showing us in picture form something about the state of our souls or about our relationship with God. For example, a Mongolian man told me of a dream which he had at regular intervals, in which he was searching on the steppe for a spring of water but could not find it. In this case, I believe that God was saying that his spiritual life was dry and that he was searching for spiritual water. Isa Mesih spoke of this spiritual water when he said "whoever drinks the water I give him will never thirst. Indeed, the water I give him will become in him a spring of water welling up to eternal life."[69] He also said,

> "If anyone is thirsty, let him come to me and drink. Whoever believes in me, as the Scripture has said, streams of living water will flow from within him." By this he meant the Spirit, whom those who believed in him were later to receive.[70]

Sometimes God may also be warning us about what will happen in the future here in this world. In that case, we might need to pray for God to protect us, or else we might have to do something practical to prepare for what will happen. In the *Taurat* we read about how God warned the ruler of Egypt through a dream about a future famine.[71] It was through the prophet Yusuf that God explained the meaning of the dream—but the prophet also gave wise advice about how they could immediately begin to prepare for the famine by storing up grain in advance. God gave enough time for them to do something about the future event he had warned them about. It is the same for us: if God gives us a warning, we have a responsibility to act upon it here and now.

If God speaks to us through our dreams, we have the responsibility to do something about it. Perhaps we need to turn away from a sin in our lives or else do something positive and good instead. An example of someone who did not heed such a dream was the Roman governor, Pontius Pilate, to whom the Jews brought Isa Mesih with the request that he be executed.

> While Pilate was sitting on the judge's seat, his wife sent him this message: "Don't have anything to do with that innocent man, for I have suffered a great deal today in a dream because of him."[72]

To some extent something similar happened to an Uzbek woman who had spoken bitter words against her daughter for attending a meeting of those who love Isa Mesih. Then in a dream the mother saw an angel flying to her, saying, "Why have you been scolding your daughter because she goes to church?" On waking up, the mother asked her daughter to forgive her.

On another occasion this same Uzbek woman was shown in a dream something of what heaven is like. Her son recounted the dream to me, saying his mother "saw a bright light and wanted to go that way; it was so beautiful and she wanted to go there but then she heard a voice saying, 'It's still too early for you to go there'—and she woke up. After that, she understood how marvellous heaven is."

Sometimes the significance of a dream only becomes apparent later on. For example, a Uighur woman in Kazakstan saw a man's face in a dream but did not know who the man was. A month or two later she met that very person in real life. It turned out that he was a man of God who loves and follows Isa Mesih, and who speaks Uighur. As a result this Uighur woman too came into a deeper and truer relationship with God.

God can also speak to us through dreams to reveal to us more about himself. I heard an example of this from a Kazak friend of mine named Karlygash when I visited her and her husband at their home. Her name, in Kazak, means a swallow: seeing her long hair flowing down her back, tied in two pigtails, I was reminded of the forked tail of the swallow. Like the birds, traditionally the Kazak people had migrated from summer to winter pastures. I too felt like a nomad in my travels.

Karlygash told me the following story about some dreams she had once experienced:

"One night I had a vivid dream in which I saw a crowd of people all busy with the events of their lives—eating, drinking, getting married, and so on. However, from my vantage point I could see a storm gathering—with violent winds about to sweep down on all these people who were totally unaware of the danger they were in. I tried to warn them but they ignored me and carried on with what they were doing.

Then the scene changed. I found myself standing on the shore and looking at the moon in the sky overhead. However, the colour of the moon looked as if it were covered with blood. Gradually the face of the moon began to clear, revealing words written on the moon. The words were:

'Our Father in heaven, may your name be honoured,
may your kingdom come,
may your will be done on earth as it is in heaven.

Give us today our daily bread,
and forgive us our debts, as we ourselves have forgiven
our debtors.

And do not lead us into temptation, but deliver us from
the evil one.'

Karlygash woke up wondering about this dream and what
it meant. Then the next night she had exactly the same dream.
It was repeated again the third night. By then Karlygash had
learned the words of the prayer which she had seen in her
dream written on the face of the moon. She began to pray
this prayer but also wondered where it had come from. She
searched through books in a library to find such a prayer but
could not find it. Eventually she came across the *Injil* and
learned that it was the prayer which Isa Mesih had taught his
followers to pray.[73]

As she read the *Injil*, she also noticed that it explained
other details of her dream. For example, in speaking about
his coming again to judge this world, Isa Mesih said,

> "Just as it was in the days of Nuh, so also will it be in
> the days of the Son of Man. People were eating, drinking,
> marrying and being given in marriage up to the day Nuh
> entered the ark. Then the flood came and destroyed them
> all.
>
> It was the same in the days of Lut. People were eating
> and drinking, buying and selling, planting and building.
> But the day Lut left Sodom, fire and sulphur rained down
> from heaven and destroyed them all. It will be just like this
> on the day the Son of Man is revealed."[74]

The detail about the moon being covered as if by blood
only makes sense when we read the prophecy given by God
to the prophet Joel, through whom God said:

"I will produce portents both in the sky and on the
earth—blood, fire, and columns of smoke.

The sunlight will be turned to darkness
and the moon to the colour of blood,
before the day of the Lord comes—that great and
terrible day!

It will so happen that everyone who calls on the name of
the Lord will be delivered..."[75]

Immediately before these words, God also spoke through
the prophet Joel about the significance of dreams and visions
given by God's Holy Spirit. He said:

"I will pour out my Spirit on all kinds of people.
Your sons and daughters will prophesy.
Your elderly will have revelatory dreams;
your young men will see prophetic visions.
Even on male and female servants
I will pour out my Spirit in those days."[76]

This prophecy which God revealed through the prophet
Joel began to be fulfilled some centuries later, when God sent
his Holy Spirit on the followers of Isa Mesih.[77] At first other
people could not understand what was happening until it
was explained as a fulfilment of what God had prophesied
through the prophet Joel. In the same way, our dreams often
do not seem to make sense until we ask God to give us insight
into their meanings. It was only when Karlygash read the *Injil*
that she began to understand what God had been saying to
her.

Is God saying something to you through your dreams? If
so, you should pray and ask God to show you what it means.
You should also ask what your response should be. If God
is speaking to you, what changes need to take place in your
behaviour and life?

46

KYRGYZSTAN: HOSPITALITY

The *marshrutka* [minibus-taxi] from Almaty to Bishek did not pass through the village I needed to visit, so from Bishkek I had to arrange with a driver to go in a private car to a village in the region of Tokmak. Arriving at that village, we found the house and were warmly welcomed inside. The family immediately brought tea to drink and various foods to eat—and that was just as starters. Later, they brought the main meal and made sure that we had plenty to eat.

Although Central Asian people are generous in their hospitality, I was relieved that they welcomed me so warmly. The previous time I had been in Kyrgyzstan I had managed to find them at the market stall where they worked and had given them a letter from the wife's sister, whom I had met in another place. Some years before that the sister had come to know Isa Mesih as her Saviour and wanted to follow and obey him. However, her family did not understand why she loved Isa Mesih. "That is not our tradition as Dungans," they said. "You are betraying your people and not following the ways of your ancestors." One day, when she was helping her father to gather hay, suddenly her father hit her forcefully over the back with his pitchfork. A second and a third time he struck her, saying that she was a traitor to her people. Then, as she lay on the ground groaning, in pain from the blows, he seemed to have compassion on her. "Go! Get out of here—quickly!" he commanded. She lost no time in running away, not stopping to fetch any personal belongings from the house.

Now I was again visiting her relatives, waiting to see how they would respond to her letter. The wife's sister had wanted to make contact with them but had been afraid to do so. I had told her about my plans to visit Kyrgyzstan and had offered to try to do what I could to help take messages to and from her family. Now I had come to see if they had any communication for me to take back to the wife's sister.

They did not ask directly where the sister was living now because they realised that she was afraid that they might still want to hurt her. However, they explained to me that they would like to re-establish contact. Without saying explicitly that her father was sorry for what he had done, they explained that he had attacked his own daughter mainly because of what other people had been saying. It was something he had felt obliged to do, not something he had really wanted to do. I was given a letter to take back to the sister, saying that she was welcome to make contact and should not fear.

Some of us feel estranged from God, rather like this Dungan lady felt separated from her family. Just like her, we need a go-between to bring about reconciliation between the two sides. I could help her as a middle-man, but who can be the go-between if we are estranged from God himself? The *Injil* tells us about such a mediator, saying: "there is one God and one intermediary between God and humanity, Isa Mesih, himself human, who gave himself as a ransom for all...."[78]

Having come from Xinjiang, there was something about the attitude of this Dungan family which struck me as rather odd. A few generations ago, the ancestors of these Dungans had come into Kyrgyzstan from the provinces of Xinjiang, Gansu and Shaanxi in north-west China. They were now accusing their sister of not following the traditions of their ancestors. However, what faith did the people of north-west

China originally have? Xinjiang has always been a cross-roads for different traditions and ideas. Even though nowadays most Uighurs and Dungans (who in China are called Hui) are Muslims, many of them would have had ancestors who were Buddhists. For example, in the history museum in Urumchi one can see an amber statue of the Buddha among various local artefacts from Xinjiang. The former Buddhist influence is even clearer at Dunhuang in Gansu province, where many of the local people nowadays are Muslims. Visitors to the Mogao caves at Dunhuang can see ancient Buddhist frescoes and huge statues of the Buddha dating from the 4th to 14th centuries AD.

Further east in China, the beginning of the 'Silk Road' was at the ancient capital of Chang'an located close to the modern city of Xi'an. One of the museums in Xi'an is called in Chinese the 碑林博物馆 (*beilin bowuguan*—literally, "Forest of Steles" Museum). On display there are many huge stone tablets dating back many centuries, one of which (in the second hall, to the left of the entrance) was engraved in 781 AD to mark the opening of a Christian church.[79] It records how in 635 AD a Syriac-speaking Christian, probably from Persia, presented copies of the Christian scriptures to the Emperor of China, who had them translated into Chinese and allowed the news about Isa Mesih to be spread among the Chinese people. By the time this stele was written in 781 AD there were followers of Isa Mesih in all the provinces and, according to the stele, in 'a hundred cities'. Although we do not know the total number of followers of Isa Mesih in China at that time, it must have been very substantial if they were to be found in a hundred cities. At that time, when Islam was not yet widespread among the ancestors of the Dungan people, it is possible that some of them were followers of Isa Mesih.[80]

Going back even further, what was the faith of the earliest Chinese people, as far as we can ascertain? More than three thousand years ago, the ancient Chinese were focussing their worship on a supreme Creator God whom they called 'Shang Di' (上帝)—the 'Sovereign Above'—and who was also referred to by the title 'Tian' (天), meaning 'Heaven'.[81] In China, as in some other parts of the world, there has been a fluctuation over time between the worship of the original creator God and the worship of other deities. The name 'Shang Di' is really a title, just as is the meaning of many of the names of God in various different languages. What is important is that those who worship and serve the creator God do not turn aside from him to serve other spirits. It seemed to me that my Dungan friend was truly following in the tradition of her ancestors and had a real and genuine love for the God who is the creator of all people.

Travelling by taxi back to Bishkek, we passed a point in the road near to a border crossing into Kazakstan. I noticed a crowd of people still standing around next to the road, though perhaps somewhat fewer than a few hours previously. My driver explained that they were waiting for someone to come along and employ them to work that day. It reminded me of a story which Isa Mesih told about men who were waiting around for most of the day before someone employed them—but they were still paid the same wage as those who had been working all the day. Those who had worked longer complained about the employer's generosity towards the others.[82] Isa Mesih told this story to show that God treats us more generously than we deserve. It is not on the basis of how much we have done that God welcomes us into heaven, but on the basis of his generosity to those who do not deserve it.

I feel sometimes the same way about the generous hospitality of people in Central Asia—that I do not deserve all that they lavish upon me. This is something which my own people in Europe can learn from the people of Central Asia, as in this regard the peoples of Central Asia and the Caucasus are closer to the culture of the Bible than are many Western Europeans and Americans. God himself also esteems this quality in the peoples of the Caucasus and Central Asia. In the Holy Book it is written:

> Share with God's people who are in need. Practice hospitality.[83]

> Offer hospitality to one another without grumbling.[84]

Another interesting verse says:

> Do not forget to entertain strangers, for by so doing some people have entertained angels without knowing it.[85]

Perhaps somewhere among the warmly hospitable people of Central Asia or the Caucasus there might be some who have entertained angels without knowing it! One example we do know about is the great prophet Ibrahim. He welcomed guests and later realised that they were angels sent from God! The *Taurat* tells us how it happened:

> The Lord appeared to Ibrahim by the oaks of Mamre while he was sitting at the entrance to his tent during the hottest time of the day. Ibrahim looked up and saw three men standing across from him. When he saw them he ran from the entrance of the tent to meet them and bowed low to the ground. He said, "My lord, if I have found favour in your sight, do not pass by and leave your servant. Let a little water be brought so that you may all wash your feet and rest under the tree. And let me get a bit of food so that you may refresh yourselves since you have passed by your servant's home. After that you may be on your way."

> "All right," they replied, "you may do as you say."

So Ibrahim hurried into the tent and said to Sarah, "Quick! Take three measures of fine flour, knead it, and make bread." Then Ibrahim ran to the herd and chose a fine, tender calf, and gave it to a servant, who quickly prepared it. Ibrahim then took some curds and milk, along with the calf that had been prepared, and placed the food before them. They ate while he was standing near them under a tree.

Then they asked him, "Where is Sarah your wife?" He replied, "There, in the tent." One of them said, "I will surely return to you when the season comes round again, and your wife Sarah will have a son!" (Now Sarah was listening at the entrance to the tent, not far behind him. Ibrahim and Sarah were old and advancing in years; Sarah had long since passed menopause.) So Sarah laughed to herself, thinking, "After I am worn out will I have pleasure, especially when my husband is old too?"

The Lord said to Ibrahim, "Why did Sarah laugh and say, 'Will I really have a child when I am old?' Is anything impossible for the Lord? I will return to you when the season comes round again and Sarah will have a son."[86]

Nowadays the descendants of the son whom God promised to Ibrahim and Sarah remember Ibrahim as an example of someone who was very hospitable. In their prayers, Jewish people pray that in their hospitality they might be more like Ibrahim.

However, the Jewish people also remember the times when God was the one who provided the food for them. It was as if God was the host and the descendants of Ibrahim were the guests! The descendants of Ibrahim had become slaves in Egypt but God had set them free from slavery. He wanted them to come to worship him and to get to know the God of their ancestors. God sent the prophet Musa to bring the descendants of Ibrahim to a place where they could meet with God. Where was this? It was in the desert—where there was no food! They grumbled about this because they did not realise that God also shows generous hospitality! If God invites us into his presence he will also provide for us the food which we need. The *Taurat* describes the hospitality of God:

> The Lord said to Musa, "I am going to rain bread from heaven for you, and the people will go out and gather the amount for each day, so that I may test them. Will they walk in my law or not? On the sixth day they will prepare what they bring in, and it will be twice as much as they gather every other day."

> ... In the evening the quail came up and covered the camp, and in the morning a layer of dew was all around the camp. When the layer of dew had evaporated, there on the surface of the desert was a thin flaky substance, thin like frost on the earth. When the Israelites saw it, they said to one another, "What is it?" because they did not know what it was.

> Musa said to them, "It is the bread that the Lord has given you for food. This is what the Lord has commanded: 'Each person is to gather from it what he can eat, an omer per person according to the number of your people; each one will pick it up for whoever lives in his tent.'"

> The Israelites did so, and they gathered – some more, some less. When they measured with an omer, the one who gathered much had nothing left over, and the one who gathered little lacked nothing; each one had gathered what he could eat.

> ...So they gathered it each morning, each person according to what he could eat, and when the sun got hot, it would melt. And on the sixth day they gathered twice

as much food, two omers per person; and all the leaders of the community came and told Musa. He said to them, "This is what the Lord has said: 'Tomorrow is a time of cessation from work, a holy Sabbath to the Lord. Whatever you want to bake, bake today; whatever you want to boil, boil today; whatever is left put aside for yourselves to be kept until morning.'"

So they put it aside until the morning, just as Musa had commanded, and it did not stink, nor were there any worms in it. Musa said, "Eat it today, for today is a Sabbath to the Lord; today you will not find it in the area. Six days you will gather it, but on the seventh day, the Sabbath, there will not be any."

On the seventh day some of the people went out to gather it, but they found nothing. So the Lord said to Musa, "How long do you refuse to obey my commandments and my instructions? See, because the Lord has given you the Sabbath, that is why he is giving you food for two days on the sixth day. Each of you stay where you are; let no one go out of his place on the seventh day." So the people rested on the seventh day.

The house of Israel called its name "manna." It was like coriander seed and was white, and it tasted like wafers with honey.

...The Israelites ate manna forty years, until they came to a land that was inhabited; they ate manna until they came to the border of the land of Canaan.[87]

For forty years Ibrahim's descendants enjoyed God's miraculous hospitality!

This miraculous bread was God's provision for them in the desert until they came into the land to which God was leading them. This is a picture of what God wants for us today too. Like the descendants of Ibrahim, we too are on a pilgrimage to the land promised by God to those who love him. On the way, God wants to nourish us with his special bread—the bread of life. With the bread of life God feeds us in our spirits and makes us spiritually strong.

These thoughts were going through my mind as I travelled back towards Bishkek. At times I chatted a little with the car driver, who had also enjoyed the Dungan family's warm hospitality and had heard why I had gone to visit them. I asked him to take me to a village near to Bishkek, where I was enjoying the warm hospitality of a Kyrgyz family. They lived in a simple village house without the conveniences of a hotel but I preferred to stay with them because of the warm and friendly atmosphere of the household. As time went on, I felt that I was being welcomed like a member of the family, rather than simply as a guest. Of course, members of the family also have to share in the work—so my practical education was broadened on another occasion when Bermet taught me how to milk their cow!

Moreover, I wanted to experience what life is like for ordinary Kyrgyz people. As I like to learn about other cultures, it is important to understand the culture at first hand by sharing in people's lives as far as I can. I am not very good at construction and practical repair jobs, so what I could do was rather limited when the family invited various relatives and friends around to help with building an extension to their house. Nevertheless, I did what I could to help. I also understood how this is a part of traditional culture: those who help with a job on one occasion can expect such help in return when they need it themselves. It is much more community-orientated than life in Western Europe. However, I think that in many ways it is closer to what God wants for us.

Kuvanich-bek and Bermet, and their family, are generous and warm-hearted people. At first, I did not know that they had any kind of faith. Later, however, Bermet invited me to go with them to a meeting in Bishkek where a large crowd of people were meeting in a stadium to hear the word of God and to receive prayer for healing and other things. When I realised how much Bermet loved God, I understood how her generous attitude is a result of her knowing how generous God has been to her.

How generous is God? This is something which I had been discussing with Ali in Xinjiang, but I was reminded of an incident in the life of Isa Mesih which shows us how generous God can be, by giving us far more than we expect:

> Isa went away to the other side of the Sea of Galilee (also called the Sea of Tiberias). A large crowd was following him because they were observing the miraculous signs he was performing on the sick. So Isa went on up the mountainside and sat down there with his disciples. (Now the Jewish feast of the Passover was near.)
>
> Then Isa, when he looked up and saw that a large crowd was coming to him, said to Philip, "Where can we buy bread so that these people may eat?" (Now Isa said this to test him, for he knew what he was going to do.)
>
> Philip replied, "Two hundred silver coins worth of bread would not be enough for them, for each one to get a little."
>
> One of Isa's disciples, Andrew, Simon Peter's brother, said to him, "Here is a boy who has five barley loaves and two fish, but what good are these for so many people?"
>
> Isa said, "Have the people sit down." (Now there was a lot of grass in that place.) So the men sat down, about five thousand in number. Then Isa took the loaves, and when

56

he had given thanks, he distributed the bread to those who were seated. He then did the same with the fish, as much as they wanted.

When they were all satisfied, Isa said to his disciples, "Gather up the broken pieces that are left over, so that nothing is wasted." So they gathered them up and filled twelve baskets with broken pieces from the five barley loaves left over by the people who had eaten. [88]

Later on, the people came searching for Isa Mesih because they wanted free food for their stomachs. However, Isa Mesih said to them:

"I tell you the solemn truth, you are looking for me not because you saw miraculous signs, but because you ate all the loaves of bread you wanted. Do not work for the food that disappears, but for the food that remains to eternal life – the food which the Son of Man will give to you. For God the Father has put his seal of approval on him.

So then they said to him, "What must we do to accomplish the deeds God requires?"

Isa replied, "This is the deed God requires – to believe in the one whom he sent."

So they said to him, "Then what miraculous sign will you perform, so that we may see it and believe you? What will you do? Our ancestors ate the manna in the wilderness, just as it is written, 'He gave them bread from heaven to eat.'"

Then Isa told them, "I tell you the solemn truth, it is not Musa who has given you the bread from heaven, but my Father is giving you the true bread from heaven. For the bread of God is the one who comes down from heaven and gives life to the world."

So they said to him, "Sir, give us this bread all the time!"

Isa said to them, "I am the bread of life. The one who comes to me will never go hungry, and the one who believes in me will never be thirsty. But I told you that you have seen me and still do not believe. Everyone whom the Father gives me will come to me, and the one who comes to me I will never send away. For I have come down from heaven not to do my own will but the will of the one who sent me. Now this is the will of the one who sent me – that I should not lose one person of every one he has given me, but raise them all up at the last day. For this is the will of my Father – for everyone who looks on the Son and believes in him to have eternal life, and I will raise him up at the last day." [89]

This means that God's hospitality is eternal! Even though the hospitality I experienced in Kyrgyzstan from these Dungan and Kyrgyz families was warm and generous, it was nevertheless temporary. Eventually I was to continue my journey. However, for each one of us the journey of life will eventually end with a meeting with God himself. What will happen then?

A hint about the future—for some people at least—is given by the prophet Isaiah, who mentioned a feast which God has prepared. He said:

On this mountain the LORD Almighty will prepare a feast of rich food for all peoples.[90]

Isa Mesih also said:

I say to you that many will come from the east and the west, and will take their places at the feast with Ibrahim, Isaak and Yakub in the kingdom of heaven.[91]

Why did Isa Mesih say that many would come "from the east and the west"? He said these words when someone who was not a descendant of the prophet Ibrahim showed even greater faith than that which Isa Mesih had seen among the Jewish people. Therefore anyone who has a sincere faith in God and wants to do God's will can be invited to share in God's eternal hospitality.

Isa Mesih gives an invitation to us now to welcome him as our guest. He said:

> Here I am! I stand at the door and knock. If anyone hears my voice and opens the door, I will come in and eat with him, and he with me.[92]

If we invite Isa Mesih to share in our lives now, we will discover that his hospitality is far more generous than anything we can give. Those who welcome Isa Mesih to share in their lives are also invited to share in the celebration feast which he has prepared for all eternity.

KYRGYZSTAN: CIRCUMCISION

While I was staying with my Kyrgyz friends in the Bishkek region, they invited me to go with them to Cholpon-Ata, on the shore of Issyk-kul, where they were visiting relatives. As I looked out over the lake at night, I could see the snow-capped mountains surrounding it like diamonds set in a ring around the lake's deep sapphire. Sparkling above us in the clear mountain air were myriads of other gems—a sky resplendent with stars—far more than I had ever been able to see elsewhere. It made me think of God's promise to the prophet Ibrahim that his descendants would be as many as the stars in the sky.[93]

The next day, Bermet said to me, "Would you like to go with us to a banquet this evening? Some friends of ours are celebrating their son's circumcision."

After we arrived at the banqueting hall, I was introduced to our hosts and to their son. The young Kyrgyz boy was dressed in his best clothes for the celebration but he was not smiling. Obviously he was still in pain. More than two hundred people had gathered for the party to celebrate his circumcision. People ate and drank, and some danced. The hosts stood up to thank all who had come. Several people made short speeches to wish the boy and the family well. However, most of them avoided mentioning the circumcision itself and none of them referred to its actual meaning.

At the table where I was seated, I turned to the man next to me and asked him what the ceremony actually means and why it is performed. He explained that it was an old custom but he did not know its meaning. I began to ask some of the others. There were three types of replies given.

Some said, "It is a sign that he is Kyrgyz."

Others said, "It makes the boy into a Muslim."

Still others said, "It's just an old tradition; I don't know why we do it."[94]

I was surprised that none of the people I asked about it knew where the custom had come from.

Suddenly I heard the *tamada* (master of ceremonies) saying into the microphone, "We have a friend here from Ireland and would like to give him an opportunity to say a few words." I obediently got up from my seat and went to the front, wondering what I should say.[95]

"Thank you. I am very glad to be here, and I want to pass on my sincere congratulations to the family on this occasion," I said. Pausing, and wondering what to say next, I turned to the *tamada* and said, "It seems to me that many people do not really know where the custom of circumcision comes from. Would you like me to tell you?"

"Certainly, go ahead," invited the *tamada*.

"The practice of circumcision comes from the prophet Ibrahim, who lived almost 4,000 years ago in what is now Iraq," I said.[96]

"Go on, tell us more," invited the *tamada*, so I began to tell them the story.

God said to the prophet Ibrahim, 'Leave your country, your people and your father's household and go to the land I will show you.

I will make you into a great nation
and I will bless you;
I will make your name great,
and you will be a blessing.

I will bless those who bless you,
and whoever curses you I will curse;
and all peoples on earth
will be blessed through you.'[97]

For a while the prophet Ibrahim settled in the town of Haran, which is now in eastern Turkey.[98] However, when he was seventy-five years old he migrated further, to the land which nowadays is called Israel. There God appeared to the prophet Ibrahim and said, 'To your descendants I will give this land.'[99]

Think about this situation! God was speaking to a seventy-five year old man who had no children. To such a man God was saying, 'I will make you into a great nation' and 'To your descendants I will give this land'! Ibrahim was known as a man of great faith but of course he must have wondered how God was going to fulfil such promises when he and his wife were both elderly and unlikely to have any children.

Later on, Ibrahim asked God this very question. He said to God,

'O Sovereign LORD, what can you give me since I remain childless and the one who will inherit my estate is Eliezer of Damascus?' And Ibrahim said, 'You have given me no children; so a servant in my household will be my heir.'

> Then the word of the LORD came to him: 'This man will not be your heir, but a son coming from your own body will be your heir.' He took him outside and said, 'Look up at the heavens and count the stars—if indeed you can count them.' Then he said to him, 'So shall your offspring be.'[100]

God wanted the prophet Ibrahim to trust him. According to the *Taurat*, it was in this very circumstance that 'Ibrahim believed the LORD, and he credited it to him as righteousness.'[101] God is pleased with the kind of trust which is willing to believe God even in difficult circumstances.

In such situations all of us can go through periods of doubt. Often we try to think of ways to obtain the desired result by our own human methods. We then rationalise our methods by saying that God can make use of them to accomplish his purposes.

It was the same even for the prophet Ibrahim. Ten years had elapsed since God had promised him a child and still he and his wife Sarai were childless. That was when Ibrahim's wife came up with an idea for him to become a father. In the *Taurat* it is written:

> Now Sarai, Ibrahim's wife, had borne him no children. But she had an Egyptian maidservant named Hagar; so she said to Ibrahim, 'The LORD has kept me from having children. Go, sleep with my maidservant; perhaps I can build a family through her.' Ibrahim agreed to what Sarai said. So after Ibrahim had been living in Canaan ten years, Sarai his wife took her Egyptian maidservant Hagar and gave her to her husband to be his wife. He slept with Hagar, and she conceived.[102]

Hagar gave birth to a son, whom the prophet Ibrahim named 'Ishmael'.[103]

God had *not* told Ibrahim to have a child through another woman who was not his wife. It was *not* an act of faith. Instead, like many of us today, Ibrahim and his wife were trying to work things out in their own human way rather than trusting in the promises given to them by God. When we act according to our own human desires and reasoning, it often prevents us from hearing what God wants to say to us. As far as we know from the scriptures, the prophet Ibrahim had no more revelations from God for the next thirteen years after the birth of Ishmael.

Then, when the prophet Ibrahim was ninety-nine years old, God spoke again and said that the promises given almost a quarter of a century previously would indeed be fulfilled—but *not* through Ishmael. God's plan was that Ibrahim's own wife Sarai should become pregnant and give birth to the child God had promised.

God said:

> 'I am the sovereign God. Walk before me and be blameless. Then I will confirm my covenant between me and you, and I will give you a multitude of descendants....'[104]

> 'As for me, this is my covenant with you: You will be the father of a multitude of nations... I will make you extremely fruitful. I will make nations of you, and kings will descend from you. I will confirm my covenant as a perpetual covenant between me and you. It will extend to your descendants after you throughout their generations. I will be your God and the God of your descendants after you. I will give the whole land of Canaan – the land where you are now residing – to you and your descendants after you as a permanent possession. I will be their God.'[105]

At that time neither Ibrahim nor Ishmael were circumcised. In fact, God had never said anything at all about circumcision up till this time. However, God now told the prophet Ibrahim that he had to cut off the foreskin from that part of his body which he had used—or, rather, misused—with his slave-girl in an attempt to get a son by his own efforts. Remember that Isaak was born when Ibrahim was one hundred years old and his wife Sarah was ninety years old. God wanted them to realise that the child was a gift from God and had nothing to do with their own fertility. His child had been born to his wife Sarah only by God's grace and was a tangible reminder that God can be trusted and God keeps his promises. However, the prophet Ibrahim had to have an 'operation' in that part of his body which he had previously tried to use with the wrong person for the wrong purposes. That area of his life had to become fully given over to God in obedience and faith.

This also illustrates a very important principle in the way that God deals with us. What is ultimately important is not our own human efforts but the grace of God. We cannot choose the place where we are born or the hour of our death. With empty hands we came into this world and with empty hands we go into the next one. Often we think that what we obtain with our hands is due to our own efforts but it is by the grace of God that we have various talents and abilities, as well as the opportunities to develop them into useful skills and the health to put those skills into practice. When we pass into the next life, this same principle of God's grace also applies. In God's Holy Book it is written: '...by grace you are saved through faith, and this not from yourselves, it is the gift of God; it is not by works, so that no one can boast.'[106]

Circumcision reminds of this same principle not only in the life of the prophet Ibrahim but also in our own lives. We too do not deserve God's mercy and kindness but the most important things in life are from God's good gifts and not the result of our own human efforts and manipulation.

God said to the prophet Ibrahim:

> 'As for you, you must keep my covenant, you and your descendants after you for the generations to come. This is my covenant with you and your descendants after you, the covenant you are to keep: Every male among you shall be circumcised. You are to undergo circumcision, and it will be the sign of the covenant between me and you. For the generations to come every male among you who is eight days old must be circumcised, including those born in your household or bought with money from a foreigner—those who are not your offspring. Whether born in your household or bought with your money, they must be circumcised. My covenant in your flesh is to be an everlasting covenant. Any uncircumcised male, who has not been circumcised in the flesh, will be cut off from his people; he has broken my covenant.'

> God also said to Ibrahim, 'As for Sarai your wife, you are no longer to call her Sarai; her name will be Sarah. I will bless her and will surely give you a son by her. I will bless her so that she will be the mother of nations; kings of peoples will come from her.'[107]

What was Ibrahim's reaction to this? We read that he laughed and said to himself:

> 'Will a son be born to a man a hundred years old? Will Sarah bear a child at the age of ninety?'

Instead of thanking God that his wife Sarah would at last have a child, Ibrahim instead said to God, "If only Ishmael might live under your blessing!"[108]

How did God respond to this request? He said, 'Yes, but your wife Sarah will bear you a son, and you will call him Isaak [which means, 'He laughs'].' God further said:

> 'I will establish my covenant with him as an everlasting covenant for his descendants after him. And as for Ishmael, I have heard you: I will surely bless him; I will make him fruitful and will greatly increase his numbers. He will be the father of twelve rulers, and I will make him into a great nation. But my covenant I will establish with Isaak, whom Sarah will bear to you by this time next year.'[109]

> On that very day Ibrahim took his son Ishmael and all those born in his household or bought with his money, every male in his household, and circumcised them, as God told him. Ibrahim was ninety-nine years old when he was circumcised, and his son Ishmael was thirteen; Ibrahim and his son Ishmael were both circumcised on that same day. And every male in Ibrahim's household, including those born in his household or bought from a foreigner, was circumcised with him.[110]

This is the origin of the tradition of circumcision. It was given to the prophet Ibrahim as a sign that his children and their descendants should be God's people and dedicated to God. Circumcision was a sign of the special agreement made between God and the prophet Ibrahim.

Both Ishmael, then aged thirteen years old, and Isaak, the child born to Sarah the following year, were circumcised. Through Ishmael the custom remained among the Arabs; likewise, through Isaak it was preserved among the Jews. That is why both Arabs and Jews are circumcised because they are all descendants of the prophet Ibrahim. Many centuries afterwards, the Arabs took the custom with them to the Caucasus and Central Asia, introducing the custom to Turkic and other non-Arab peoples.

That is why both Jews and Muslims practise circumcision, so we cannot say that circumcision makes a boy into a Muslim; in fact, male circumcision is not even mentioned in the Qur'an, and no explanation of the custom is given there.

Neither can we say that it makes a person into a Kyrgyz— or an Uzbek, Karakalpak, Talysh, Lak, Avar, Chechen or any other nationality. Even if most of the men of that nationality are circumcised, the fact of circumcision is not in itself what gives a person nationality or ethnic identity.

So what does circumcision mean for us today? Why should people still practise it?

The prophet Jeremiah talked about circumcision over two and a half thousand years ago, about 600 years before Isa Mesih. He mentioned a list of different ethnic groups who practised circumcision and who lived in various part of the Middle East. The prophet Jeremiah said that God was going to punish 'all who are circumcised only in the flesh' because 'all these nations are really uncircumcised' in their hearts.[111]

The prophet said that the physical ritual is meaningless if one is not circumcised in one's heart.

What, then, did the prophet Jeremiah mean about needing to be circumcised in one's heart? We too may have areas of our lives where we have tried to do things our own way, not in the way that God has ordained. If so, we need to submit those parts of our lives to God. Like the foreskin in circumcision, there needs to be a cutting away of any area of our lives which is not fully submitted to God. God can perform this 'operation' in our lives. He is the one who can 'circumcise' our hearts by cutting away the power of our sinful natures.[112]

69

It is written that the prophet Ibrahim 'received the sign of circumcision as a seal of the righteousness that he had by faith while he was still uncircumcised, so that he would become the father of all those who believe but have never been circumcised, that they too could have righteousness credited to them. And he is also the father of the circumcised, who are not only circumcised, but who also walk in the footsteps of the faith that our father Ibrahim possessed when he was still uncircumcised.'[113]

Therefore it is also written:

> Circumcision is nothing and uncircumcision is nothing. Instead, keeping God's commandments is what counts.[114]

> Neither circumcision nor uncircumcision counts for anything; the only thing that matters is a new creation![115]

How do we become a 'new creation'? This too is the work of God—as was Isaak, the child whom God gave to the prophet Ibrahim and his wife Sarah. All of us, whether male or female, can become a 'new creation' if we submit to God's operation which takes away the sin in our spirits. You too can ask God to circumcise your heart. If you would like to do this, you can say to God in your own language the following prayer:

'Holy God, I want to listen to you and to do things your way. Please forgive me for not listening to you but instead doing things my own way. I submit my whole life to you. Please cut out from my spirit all that is dirty, selfish or unworthy of you. I want to become 'circumcised' in my heart, which only you can do. Please make me a new creation. Please send your Holy Spirit to make me new and clean inside. Amen.'

TAJIKISTAN: FEAR OR LOVE?

"Aren't you afraid to travel by yourself in these regions?" asked Jamshed as he drove his car towards Khujand. We had just stopped to fill up the tank of gas which powered his car—the first time I had seen gas being used rather than petrol. Jamshed was a doctor in his thirties, although his hairline was already receding. To some extent the loss of hair on top was compensated for by his short black beard. He had stopped to pick me up from the side of the road and we had already been talking for quite a while about a variety of different topics.

"Yes, I know there are dangers, and at times I wonder what I would do," I replied. "But I am not afraid because I know that God looks after me. That doesn't mean that everything will necessarily be easy or smooth, but I trust that God's angels will protect me."

"But what if they don't?"

"Sometimes God does allow us to go through suffering," I answered, "and that is often a process of purifying us, to make us more as God wants us to be. In the end, all of us die, so we all have to be prepared for eternity. If God allows me to live a little longer, I have to trust that he still has his purposes for me here on this earth."

"I suppose it's because you are on a pilgrimage that God would look after you!"

"Sometimes terrible things happen even to those on pilgrimage."

"Yes—they can get stuck on the road—like you were today!"

"Exactly! I would not have been able to get back from the reservoir—what you called 'the sea of Tajikistan'—without you! In the same way, we all need to have someone with us on the journey of life who can show us the way and help us in times of need."

"But you were alone—which shows that you are not doing what you say you should!"

"Yes, that's what it looks like. But actually, I believe that I do have a companion who is with me all the time—and who even sent you along to help me!"

"What do you mean?"

"I mean that it is much easier if we have someone else to go with us on the path of life—and that is exactly what Isa Mesih promised to those who love him. He said to his followers, 'Surely I will be with you always, to the very end of the age.'"[116]

"How can Isa Mesih be with you? He is now in heaven with God!"

"That is true too. However, before his death and his resurrection from the dead he had said to his companions, 'Unless I go away, the Counsellor will not come to you; but if I go, I will send him to you.'[117] It is this Counsellor who is with me on the path of life."

"Who is this Counsellor you are talking about?"

"Isa Mesih described this Counsellor as follows:

'If you love me, you will obey what I command. And I will
ask the Father, and he will give you another Counsellor,
to be with you for ever—the Spirit of truth. The world
cannot accept him, because it neither sees him nor knows
him. But you know him, for he lives with you and will
be in you. I will not leave you as orphans; I will come to
you....'[118]

"If Isa Mesih said, 'I will come to you', why is he also saying
it is this Counsellor, this 'Holy Spirit', who comes to you?"

"The Holy Spirit is also described in the Holy Book as
the 'spirit of Isa'.[119] That is why he wants to change our lives
to make us more like God intended us to be. It is also why
the Holy Spirit brings to our minds God's teachings so that
we do not get lost on the journey of life. Isa Mesih said, 'The
Counsellor, the Holy Spirit, whom the Father will send in
my name, will teach you all things and will remind you of
everything I have said to you.'[120]"

"But he still let you get stuck on the road today, didn't
he?"

"Yes—until you came along! Thank you so much for your
help and for bringing me here!"

"We Tajiks say that a guest is sent from God. So I suppose
that God allowed you to be stuck so that you can come to our
home! I want to introduce you to my family."

He stopped the car in front of a large iron gate. The buildings were arranged around a central courtyard. Taking off
our shoes, we went inside. After the heat of the day, I was
glad to be in the much cooler, shaded interior. I was also glad
to have an opportunity to relax a little after travelling from
Kyrgyzstan. Even though I had flown over the mountains
from Bishkek to Dushanbe, the journey by road over the

73

pass to Khujand had been a tiring one. (Yes, pilgrims can use planes too, just as in the past they used whatever transport was available, even if only a donkey or horse!).

"This is my wife, Zarina," announced Jamshed. I respectfully greeted her before Zarina slipped away to another room.

"And who is this?" I asked, noticing a wooden cradle in the middle of the floor.

"She was born three months ago."

"What's her name?"

"Munira."

Proudly Jamshed looked down on his sleeping daughter. I refrained from commenting on how beautiful the baby looked, or praising the baby in any other way, as I knew that many people in Central Asia are afraid of the evil eye.

As if reading my thoughts, Jamshed remarked, "Look! Our baby has a spiritual companion too—just like the Holy Spirit you say is with you!"

I looked in the direction he was indicating and saw an amulet firmly attached to the infant's clothing.

"This protects our baby from the *jinn* and evil spirits which might try to attack her," explained Jamshed.

"So are you afraid of the evil eye?" I asked.

"Everyone is afraid of the evil eye. But, even if there is nothing to it, I think that it is safer to put the amulet there just in case it does help!"

"Why do you think the amulet can help?" I asked, "Do you know what the Qur'an says about the evil eye?"

"The Qur'an?" Jamshed paused, thinking, then admitted, "Sorry, I can't think what it says about the evil eye. What does it say?"

"Nothing at all!" I replied. "If you read the Qur'an, you will find nothing about the evil eye—or the need for any kind of talisman to protect against it."

"Really? But surely it must say about the evil eye, otherwise why would everyone be afraid of it and attach talismans to their children to protect against the evil eye?"

"Because what you fear is actually a popular folk belief, probably dating to before the time of Islam. It is not an official doctrine of Islam."

Jamshed thought for a moment, then commented, "I never heard it put that way before but you are probably right because, when we drop aspand seeds on hot charcoal and the smoke swirls around the child's head to ward off the evil eye, I have heard that what we say is actually a prayer not to Allah but to a dead king named Naqshband—who was not even a Muslim but a Zoroastrian, who lived before the coming of Islam! We say in Tajik:

'Aspand balla band
Ba haq shah-e-naqshband
Chashm-e-aaish chashm-e-khaysh
Chashm-e-adam-e bad andaysh
Besuzad dar atash-e-taiz'."[121]

"What does that mean?" I asked.

"I can try to translate it as something like this:

75

'This is aspand, it banishes the evil eye.
The blessing of King Naqshband
Eye of nothing, Eye of relatives
Eye of friends, Eye of enemies
Whoever is bad should burn in this glowing fire.'[122]

"When you fear the evil eye," I remarked, "what you are afraid of is a kind of curse which you think can be put on a child by someone who is jealous. Where does the power of the curse come from? Is it from God—or from evil spirits?"

"From Satan, or evil spirits like the *jinn*."

"Yes, that's right, but it is also partly because of your own fear."

"What do you mean?"

"You are a good father. I am sure that your wife, Zarina, is a good mother who cares for your baby very conscientiously—feeding her, changing her clothes, cuddling her, playing with her, doing everything that a good mother should do for her infant. Both of you want her to grow up strong and healthy. In your heart of hearts, what you would also like is for her is to be an honest, kind and faithful sort of person, whom people can respect not for what she does but for who she is."

"You are right. That is what we want for our daughter."

"But what happens if something bad does happen to her—like when you found me today on the road? I was stranded and helpless. You yourself asked me how God could have been looking after me if I'm supposed to be on a pilgrimage!"

"So what does this have to do with my little Munira and her talisman?"

"You are a father and you care for your daughter, but you also know that as she grows up in life she will experience hardships and difficulties. Don't you think that God has the same concern for us? He loves us like you love Munira—but if she does not experience difficulties in life she will be immature. God wants us to grow up too."

"But it is right for us to be concerned about our families, to do what we can to look after them and protect them."

"Yes, it is right to be concerned, but sometimes our fear for our children or fears of other things can even get in the way of knowing God in a real and meaningful way."

"How can that be? How can our fear hinder our knowing God?"

"Have you heard of the great prophet Ayoub?"

"I have heard the name but I don't know anything about him."

"Even this great prophet had the experience that what he feared actually happened. He said:

'What I feared has come upon me;
    what I dreaded has happened to me.'"[123]

"So what did the prophet Ayoub fear?" asked Jamshed.

"He was afraid about his children. We read in the Holy Book that before a series of disasters occurred the prophet Ayoub was very concerned about his children: 'His sons used to take turns holding feasts in their homes, and they would invite their three sisters to eat and drink with them. When a period of feasting had run its course, Ayoub would send and have them purified. Early in the morning he would sacrifice a burnt offering for each of them, thinking, "Perhaps my children have sinned and cursed God in their hearts." This was Ayoub's regular custom.'"[124]

"But you said that some disasters occurred. Are you saying that God allowed the great prophet Ayoub to suffer that which he had feared so much?"

"We read in the Holy Book that it was in fact Satan who attacked the prophet and caused these disasters. Satan tries to attack us in the areas of our lives where we are weakest. Why do you think it was that Satan could attack Ayoub in this way?"

"You said it was where he was weakest—but you said that he offered sacrifices so that what he feared would not happen. I suppose a sacrifice is even greater than the talisman we have put on our daughter. But are you saying that even this prophet's sacrifices did not stop the disasters?"

"That's right."

"But why?" queried Jamshed. "Why did God not stop the disasters?"

"Might it be that even the great prophet Ayoub was focussing so much on his own family that he lost sight of the loving nature of God? Ayoub feared disaster and he also feared God, but perhaps it was his fear which prevented him from knowing God more intimately. In fact, later on in the story of Ayoub, as recorded in the Holy Book, the prophet Ayoub says to God:

> 'I know that you can do all things;
>   no plan of yours can be thwarted.

You asked, "Who is this that obscures my counsel
without knowledge?"
Surely I spoke of things I did not understand,
things too wonderful for me to know.

You said, "Listen now, and I will speak;
I will question you,
and you shall answer me."

My ears had heard of you
but now my eyes have seen you.

Therefore I despise myself
and repent in dust and ashes.'"[125]

"So you are saying that what is most important in life is knowing God?"

"That's right! Ayoub had known about God with his ears but it was 'head knowledge' and he had not experienced a personal revelation of God. When God did reveal himself more fully to Ayoub, the prophet understood that his conception of God had been faulty."

"So he put his trust in his sacrifices, like we put our trust in our amulets?"

"Ayoub feared God and was afraid for his children and so he did the right religious actions, but his motivation was fear. However, it was through his experiences of suffering that he then came to understand that knowing God is far more important."

"So are you saying that, like Ayoub, we can be very religious but can still have a limited understanding of the nature of God? Can even a great prophet be like that?"

"The question is: 'What motivates our religious actions?' Is it fear? There is another motivation which is much greater than fear. If we know God more intimately, our motivations change because we understand that God cares for us deeply like a good parent."

"I try to be a good parent, but I am also afraid."

"But do you want your child to grow up fearing you?"

"No, I want her to love me, to trust me."

"And God wants the same in our relationship with him! Isa Mesih spoke of this trust in a loving God when he compared God to a good father who lavishes good gifts on his children. Isa Mesih said:

> 'Therefore I tell you, do not worry about your life, what you will eat or drink; or about your body, what you will wear. Is not life more important than food, and the body more important than clothes? Look at the birds of the air; they do not sow or reap or store away in barns, and yet your heavenly Father feeds them. Are you not much more valuable than they? Who of you by worrying can add a single hour to his life? And why do you worry about clothes? See how the lilies of the field grow. They do not labour or spin. Yet I tell you that not even Suleiman in all his splendour was dressed like one of these. If that is how God clothes the grass of the field, which is here today and tomorrow is thrown into the fire, will he not much more clothe you, O you of little faith? So do not worry, saying, "What shall we eat?" or "What shall we drink?" or "What shall we wear?" For the pagans run after all these things, and your heavenly Father knows that you need them. But seek first his kingdom and his righteousness, and all these things will be given to you as well. Therefore do not worry about tomorrow, for tomorrow will worry about itself. Each day has enough trouble of its own.'[126]

"You are saying that God loves us. But that means... it means that if God is everywhere and knows everything, it means that we have nothing to fear!"

"Exactly! If God himself is going to care for us, we do not need to rely on religious rituals—even the kinds of sacrifices which the prophet Ayoub was doing. So when God himself is present next to a child and protecting the child in person, we no longer need the amulet or any other substitute for God himself. In fact, the talisman can even be offensive to God because it is shows that we are putting our trust in a talisman and not in the living and true God."

"When we do that, can it be that God can allow us to suffer that which we had feared, so that we realise that our trust is not put in the right place? If so, my talisman is a danger rather than a help!"

"What is important is that we should trust the reality of God, who is personal, rather than the symbol which is impersonal."

"Is that what you meant on the road about your companion—your Counsellor, God's Holy Spirit? You said that he is with you all the time."

"I said that Isa Mesih promised to be with us to the end of the age. However, it is also possible for us to grieve God's Holy Spirit by doing things which are not pleasing to God."

"Just as a child can do things which grieve a parent—but we still continue to love our children even if they do grieve us by doing things they should not."

"We are like God's children. However, a child has to learn to respect his or her parents. Even though a parent loves the child, there is also a place for fear in the relationship. There is a phase in the development of a young child's understanding of right and wrong when the child needs to fear the parent's displeasure and punishment. Through that fear, the child learns to do right and to avoid wrong conduct. It is the same in our relationship with God. In the *Zabur*, the prophet Davud writes:

> 'The fear of the LORD is the beginning of wisdom;
> all who follow his precepts have good understanding.'[127]

The prophet Suleiman, who was a son of the prophet Davud, likewise wrote:

> 'The fear of the LORD is the beginning of wisdom,
> and knowledge of the Holy One is understanding.'[128]

Elsewhere, the prophet Suleiman also wrote:

> 'The fear of the LORD is the beginning of knowledge,
> but fools despise wisdom and discipline.'[129]

Therefore our fear has to be in the right place. A holy respect for God is like that of a child who fears the parent's displeasure and therefore does not want to do wrong. That is the right kind of fear."

"Fear—or love! So there is a place for healthy fear but it has to be balanced by a right understanding of God's love. Is that what you are saying?"

"Yes. Do you know what happened when God first created mankind?"

"I know he made Adam as the first man but I don't remember what else happened."

"God put Adam and Eve in the Garden of Eden, where he allowed them to eat from any tree in the garden apart from one. This one forbidden fruit was from the 'tree of the knowledge of good and evil'. Before they ate of that fruit, Adam and Eve only knew what it was like to be good. However, the day came when they chose to disobey God's instruction. After eating the forbidden fruit, they suddenly knew what it was like to experience wrongdoing as well as good. Just as children hide from their parents when they know that they have done wrong, Adam and Eve tried to hide from God. Before they ate of the forbidden fruit, they had enjoyed a close, personal friendship with God because they respected the boundaries which God had placed on them. Theirs had been the right kind of fear of God, which was the beginning of wisdom. However, when they sinned and disobeyed God, they had a fear of God's punishment because they knew they had done wrong."

"But why did they sin? Surely they wanted to have a right relationship with God?"

"Adam and Eve had been deceived by Satan. However, God continued to love them."

"So Satan deceived Adam and Eve, and Satan also wanted to attack the prophet Ayoub! If Satan is always wanting to attack us, or to send *jinn* against us, then of course we need protection from the evil eye! That is why I have my talisman!"

"But you need to hear the end of the story of Adam and Eve! There is good news too! Even when punishing them, God promised that one day he would send a Saviour who would overcome the power of Satan. In the garden of Eden, God said to Satan:

'I will put enmity between you and the woman,
and between your offspring and hers;

83

> he will crush your head,
> and you will strike his heel.'[130]

This prophecy was fulfilled in Isa Mesih, who conquered the power of Satan. Satan struck at Isa Mesih and tried to kill him by getting sinful human beings to crucify him. However, Isa Mesih was without sin, and through his death he took on himself the punishment which he did not deserve, but which we deserve. God then raised Isa Mesih to life and crowned him with glory and honour. In this way, Isa Mesih crushed Satan's head. If we belong to Isa Mesih, we too can share in this victory over Satan.

Therefore, if we belong to Isa Mesih, we do not have to fear the powers of darkness. There is no need to fear the evil eye. Talismans and amulets are worthless because only the power of God has authority over the jinn and evil spirits. Isa Mesih has defeated those powers of darkness so we need to call on the name of Isa Mesih when we want the powers of darkness to flee. To those who belong to him, Isa Mesih promised that in his name they would drive out demons.[131] This authority is given to those who truly know and follow Isa Mesih and are filled with his Holy Spirit."

"Isa Mesih has power to drive out the evil spirits!" exclaimed Jamshed. "Can he also break the curse of the evil eye? I want that kind of power if it is available to me and to my children!"

"Nothing can separate us from God's love if we belong to Isa Mesih. In the *Injil* it is written: 'For I am convinced that neither death nor life, neither angels nor demons, neither the present nor the future, nor any powers, neither height nor depth, nor anything else in all creation, will be able to separate us from the love of God that is in Isa Mesih our Lord.'[132]

That is also why the *Injil* says: 'God is love. Whoever lives in love lives in God, and God in him. In this way, love is made complete among us so that we will have confidence on the day of judgment, because in this world we are like him. There is no fear in love. But perfect love drives out fear, because fear has to do with punishment. The one who fears is not made perfect in love.'"[133]

"I know that I often fear," admitted Jamshed. "But if the perfect love of God drives out fear, I want that! If God's perfect love drives out fear, then my fears show that I am not really trusting the God who loves me. I suppose I am like the prophet Ayoub: I have been trusting in my religious acts rather than knowing God in a personal way. I've been trusting in religious symbols such as amulets rather than trusting in the loving nature of God."

"Do you want to turn away from your misplaced trust in the symbols and put your real trust in God himself? If this is something you would like to do, all you need to do is to tell God that, and to ask him to change you so that you have the right motivations."

Suddenly, Jamshed was on his knees, talking to God in a way like he had never spoken with God before. From his heart came words which he had not been taught by another person but which flowed from inside himself. He was saying, "Lord God, I confess that I have been motivated by fear rather than by love. Because of my fears, I have been doing religious acts and good deeds but I have not done it for the right motivations. I want to be motivated not by fear but by love. Please take away my wrong motivations and forgive me for them. I ask that you give me a new revelation of your love for me, so that I may know you better. Please reveal your loving heart to me—your love for people, which is like the love of a parent for a child. I know that you love me and care for me, and I want to experience your Father love, which takes away fear. Help me to get to know you in a sincere and true way."

TAJIKISTAN: LIVING WITH LOSS

"You told me that the prophet Ayoub suffered disasters, but I don't suppose they were anything like the way our family has suffered," remarked Jamshed. I was still staying at his home and he was interested in pursuing the discussion further.

"How has your family suffered?" I asked.

"My younger brother was killed in the civil war. It was not his fault: he was just visiting some friends when a bomb went off and he got killed. Then three years ago I was in the Pamirs with my two teenage sons. Suddenly, there was a terrible rumbling noise above us—a landslide. I shouted, 'Run!' but both of them got hit on their heads by the falling rocks. I tried to do what I could to help, but they both died."

Jamshed burst into tears at the memory of his lost sons. I did not know what to say but simply put my arm round his shoulder. I was moved and felt almost like weeping too.

A few minutes passed. Then, suddenly, Jamshed raised his eyes and said, "Why should God allow such things to happen? Was he punishing us for something?"

"Really, I do not know all the answers," I replied. "Sometimes it might be that God allows it, but often it can actually be the work of Satan, who comes to kill and destroy—and also to steal.[134] I cannot be sure what the reason was in your particular case."

"At one time, I felt angry with God for letting this happen," Jamshed whispered, slowly. Then, his voice a little louder, he said, "But now I realise that we cannot understand the mind of God and perhaps Satan was responsible."

"You are right," I said, "because there are many things we do not know about what is really going on in the unseen realms. We get a glimpse of things in this world but there are many hidden things."

I paused, not sure how much it was appropriate to say. Jamshed needed comfort, not an intellectual discussion about suffering. My eyes fell on his beautiful wall covering—a tapestry or carpet which filled most of the wall in front of us.

Jamshed lifted his head and looked at me. He seemed to be composing himself.

"Would you like a cup of tea?" I suggested.

"Not just now," he replied. Then he seemed to remember the remark he had made earlier.

"So what did happen to the prophet Ayoub?" he asked.

"He also suffered the loss of children, just like you have." I replied, "But do you really want to hear about it now? I can tell you another time if you prefer."

"Don't worry about me! I often cry when I think of my sons. But tell me how the prophet Ayoub coped with his loss. Perhaps that might help me in my grief too."

"All right, then, if you're sure you want to hear."

"Yes, tell me."

"You remember that yesterday I said that what he feared actually came upon him. Even prophets can fear and make mistakes. Do you know why he was a great prophet?"

"No. Was it because of wonderful miracles in his life? Maybe something like those God did through the prophets Musa or Isa Mesih?"

"No—as far as we know, the prophet Ayoub did not experience those kinds of miracles. It was a much simpler reason—and something which we all can relate to in some way. The reason the prophet Ayoub was so great was because of the way he coped with suffering and loss—even though he did not understand why terrible events were happening in his life."

"Really? How did he cope with his loss or sufferings?"

"Can I read to you what the Holy Book says about it?"

"Please do."

I started to read: 'In the land of Uz there lived a man whose name was Ayoub. This man was blameless and upright; he feared God and shunned evil. He had seven sons and three daughters, and he owned seven thousand sheep, three thousand camels, five hundred yoke of oxen and five hundred donkeys, and had a large number of servants. He was the greatest man among all the people of the East....'[135]."

"Where did he live?" interjected Jamshed, "Did you say Uzbekistan?"

"No—not Uzbekistan, although I've heard some people think it might be in Central Asia! It was somewhere in the Middle East, perhaps where the modern country of Jordan is, from what we can tell from references to it by another prophet."[136]

"OK—I just wondered. In any case, he sounds rather like a rich Central Asian! Please carry on."

"One day," I continued reading, "the angels came to present themselves before the LORD, and Satan also came with them. The LORD said to Satan, 'Where have you come from?'

> Satan answered the LORD, 'From roaming through the earth and going back and forth in it.'

> Then the LORD said to Satan, 'Have you considered my servant Ayoub? There is no one on earth like him; he is blameless and upright, a man who fears God and shuns evil.'

> 'Does Ayoub fear God for nothing?' Satan replied. 'Have you not put a hedge around him and his household and everything he has? You have blessed the work of his hands, so that his flocks and herds are spread throughout the land. But stretch out your hand and strike everything he has, and he will surely curse you to your face.'

> The LORD said to Satan, 'Very well, then, everything he has is in your hands, but on the man himself do not lay a finger.' Then Satan went out from the presence of the LORD...."[137]

"So what did Satan do to Ayoub?" asked Jamshed.

"Satan caused a series of disasters to befall the prophet's family and possessions. In a single day, he lost all his children and all his livestock."

"All his children? How many did he have?"

"Seven sons and three daughters."

"And all ten of them were killed! How terrible! What happened?"

"A messenger came to the prophet Ayoub and told him, 'Your sons and daughters were feasting and drinking wine at the oldest brother's house, when suddenly a mighty wind swept in from the desert and struck the four corners of the house. It collapsed on them and they are dead...'[138] This was on top of other disasters in which the prophet's livestock were killed, or were stolen by enemy raiders, and most of his servants were also killed apart from the ones who survived to bring him the news."[139]

"But surely God could have stopped Satan doing these things?" queried Jamshed.

"Yes, you are right: God does have that power. For example, it seems that Satan later on tried to kill Isa Mesih in a similar way, by sending a strong wind while he was asleep in a boat—but Isa Mesih was able to command the wind and waves to be still.[140] However, in the case of the prophet Ayoub God was not going to go back on his word even to Satan. I can only assume that the prophet's children went to heaven and that eventually Ayoub was re-united with them—so in that sense the loss was temporary."

"All right, I understand that we do not know all the reasons. Carry on reading from the Holy Book. How did the prophet Ayoub cope with these terrible disasters?"

"At this, Ayoub got up and tore his robe and shaved his head," I read, "Then he fell to the ground in worship and said:

'Naked I came from my mother's womb,
and naked I will depart.
The LORD gave and the LORD has taken away;
may the name of the LORD be praised.'

In all this, Ayoub did not sin by charging God with wrongdoing."[141]

"It must have been very hard to suffer such a serious loss," remarked Jamshed, "losing one's children and possessions all on the same day. It is like the loss which some people suffer during a war or in a disaster like an earthquake or tsunami."

"You are right," I agreed, "But, more than that, the prophet Ayoub did not know anything about the unseen powers which were behind these terrible events. That is why the experience of the prophet Ayoub is so relevant for our lives. We too can learn from his experience how to cope with loss in our lives. It also gives us a hint that perhaps there is an even greater, unseen spiritual conflict going on around us which may be affecting our lives too."

"So what happened next?"

"Things got even worse for the man of God. We read:

On another day the angels came to present themselves before the LORD, and Satan also came with them to present himself before him. And the LORD said to Satan, "Where have you come from?"

Satan answered the LORD, "From roaming through the earth and going back and forth in it."

Then the LORD said to Satan, "Have you considered my servant Ayoub? There is no one on earth like him; he is blameless and upright, a man who fears God and shuns evil. And he still maintains his integrity, though you incited me against him to ruin him without any reason."

"Skin for skin!" Satan replied. "A man will give all he has for his own life. But stretch out your hand and strike his flesh and bones, and he will surely curse you to your face."

92

The LORD said to Satan, "Very well, then, he is in your hands; but you must spare his life."

So Satan went out from the presence of the LORD and afflicted Ayoub with painful sores from the soles of his feet to the top of his head. Then Ayoub took a piece of broken pottery and scraped himself with it as he sat among the ashes.

His wife said to him, "Are you still holding on to your integrity? Curse God and die!"

He replied, "You are talking like a foolish woman. Shall we accept good from God, and not trouble?" In all this, Ayoub did not sin in what he said.[142]

The prophet Ayoub did not blame God for his sufferings, but he too was thinking deeply about why he was suffering in this way. If we look only at the material, visible events they seem unfair and we cannot make sense of them."

"I understand what you are saying, but it is hard to come to terms with such things if we can see only the physical, material events."

"That's true too. It was the same when some of the prophet's friends heard about what had happened to him and came to visit him. They were appalled at what they saw and they too did not know how to explain it. They thought that a religious person like Ayoub ought to live a happy and prosperous life as a sign of God's blessing."

"Many people today also think like that," commented Jamshed. "They say that if someone is suffering, it must be a sign that the person has sinned, so it is the person's own fault. For example, Hindus and Buddhists say that if a person is born crippled or blind, or in a poor or low-caste family, it is the person's own fault, because of sins done in a previous existence. If you put the blame on someone like that, you tend not to have much compassion for the afflicted person."

"That's very perceptive, I think! Certainly the prophet's friends seemed to think that way. Centuries later, at the time of Isa Mesih, people also thought that illness must be the result of a person's sin. Isa Mesih had a totally different attitude, however."

"In what way?"

"We read in the *Injil* the following account about Isa Mesih:

> 'As Isa was passing by, he saw a man who had been blind from birth. His disciples asked him, "Rabbi, who committed the sin that caused him to be born blind, this man or his parents?" Isa answered, "Neither this man nor his parents sinned, but he was born blind so that the acts of God may be revealed through what happens to him. We must perform the deeds of the one who sent me as long as it is daytime. Night is coming when no one can work. As long as I am in the world, I am the light of the world." Having said this, he spat on the ground and made some mud with the saliva. He smeared the mud on the blind man's eyes and said to him, "Go wash in the pool of Siloam" (which is translated "sent"). So the blind man went away and washed, and came back seeing.'[143]

"So he healed the blind man!" exclaimed Jamshed. "He did not just accept suffering but he did something about it!"

"Yes. I would suggest that the proper response to suffering is compassion. If possible, we should do something about it. It was compassion which motivated Isa Mesih to heal sick and suffering people. We read: Isa 'went throughout all the towns and villages, teaching in their synagogues, preaching the good news of the kingdom, and healing every kind of disease and sickness. When he saw the crowds, he had compassion on them, because they were bewildered and helpless, like sheep without a shepherd.'"[144]

"That is different from the friends of the prophet Ayoub, who thought that suffering must be a result of sin."

"Indeed. Their lack of empathy and true compassion began to show itself, as they tried to justify the prophet's suffering by saying that Ayoub himself must have sinned. The prophet's so-called 'comforters' knew some truth but they thought it was the whole truth. We all know that some suffering does come from sin—whether our own sin or that of another person which affects us. However, this is not the whole story."

"So how did the story of the prophet Ayoub end?" asked Jamshed.

"In the end, God himself intervened and spoke to them all. God did not provide all the answers but showed them that there is a much 'bigger picture' than our finite human minds can comprehend. The prophet Ayoub acknowledged before God that he had spoken of things he did not understand.[145] God then spoke directly to one of the prophet's friends and said, 'I am angry with you and your two friends, because you have not spoken of me what is right, as my servant Ayoub has.'"[146]

"God calls Ayoub his servant. Why doesn't he call Ayoub his prophet?"

"Even though God himself confirmed that Ayoub had spoken 'what is right' about God, this in itself does not mean that we can say that Ayoub was a 'prophet'! A prophet is someone who not only speaks what is right about God but is also a messenger of God, who communicates to other people what he has received by revelation from God."

"And did Ayoub do this too?"

"Yes, indeed! Ayoub had a deep insight into spiritual truths which he must have received by revelation from the Most High. Ayoub said:

> 'I know that my Redeemer lives,
> and that in the end he will stand upon the earth.
>
> And after my skin has been destroyed,
> yet in my flesh I will see God;
>
> I myself will see him
> with my own eyes—I, and not another.
> How my heart yearns within me!'[147]

This was a deep truth which Ayoub could only have received by revelation from God."

"But who was the prophet Ayoub talking about? Who is this Redeemer who in the end will stand upon the earth?" queried Jamshed. "And why a Redeemer?"

"The prophet Ayoub knew that he had a deliverer who would set free or rescue or ransom him. However, to redeem something is to buy it back—to recover ownership by paying a specified sum. Who do you think might be willing to do this for Ayoub? What do you think was the price which had to be paid? Why did Ayoub have to look forward to a time when his Redeemer would stand upon the earth?"

"I suspect that you want to say it is Isa Mesih—but the prophet Ayoub lived almost as many years before the time of Isa Mesih as we live after his time."

"Exactly! That is why his prophecy is so amazing: God knew so far in advance what he was going to do! We can see a fulfilment of Ayoub's prophecy as expressed in the following words from the *Injil*:

> The grace of God has appeared, bringing salvation to all people. It trains us to reject godless ways and worldly desires and to live self-controlled, upright, and godly lives in the present age, as we wait for the happy fulfillment of our hope in the glorious appearing of our great God and Saviour, Isa Mesih. He gave himself for us to set us free from every kind of lawlessness and to purify for himself a people who are truly his, who are eager to do good."[148]

"So you mean that the prophet Ayoub's words were fulfilled by Isa Mesih?"

"Definitely! In fact, Isa Mesih said of himself, 'even the Son of Man did not come to be served, but to serve, and to give his life as a ransom for many.'"[149]

"What do you mean by 'even the Son of Man' came to give his life as a ransom for many? Who is this 'Son of Man'?"

"Isa Mesih often used this term when referring to himself. Those who heard him would be reminded of the prophetic vision which the prophet Daniel had seen and which described someone 'like a son of man' who would rule all the nations."

"Really? I've heard of the prophet Daniel. In fact, they say that the prophet Daniel's tomb is in Uzbekistan! What did he see?"

"Would you like me to read it to you?" I picked up my Bible and read from the seventh chapter of the book of Daniel:

> 'In my vision at night I looked, and there before me was one like a son of man, coming with the clouds of heaven.

He approached the Ancient of Days and was led into his presence. He was given authority, glory and sovereign power; all peoples, nations and men of every language worshipped him. His dominion is an everlasting dominion that will not pass away, and his kingdom is one that will never be destroyed.'[150]

"So you mean that Isa Mesih was claiming to be such a king?" asked Jamshed, amazed.

"Indirectly, yes, but he also explained that his kingdom is not of this world.[151] He did not want people to think he was going to lead a rebellion against the Romans. In fact, the way the Jews managed to get the Romans to put Isa to death was on the grounds of his claiming to be a king. The Jews at that time were expecting someone they called the 'Anointed One'—that is the meaning of the term 'Mesih' or 'Messiah', which in Greek was 'Christos'. However, they thought this would be a conquering political ruler who would liberate the Jews from the Romans. They did not understand that Isa Mesih came to set them free from the much more dangerous one in whose power they actually were held captive—that is, Satan."

"But people call him Isa Mesih or Jesus Christ. Didn't he call himself that?"

"Usually he avoided that title to avoid misunderstandings but he did occasionally say it more directly. Actually, that was why the Jewish authorities wanted to kill him, because he was claiming to be the one sent from God."

"What did he say?"

In answer, I read the following passage from the *Injil*:

The high priest said to him, "I charge you under oath by the living God: Tell us if you are the Mesih, the Son of God."

"Yes, it is as you say," Isa replied. "But I say to all of you: In the future you will see the Son of Man sitting at the right hand of the Mighty One and coming on the clouds of heaven."

Then the high priest tore his clothes and said, "He has spoken blasphemy! Why do we need any more witnesses? Look, now you have heard the blasphemy. What do you think?"

"He is worthy of death," they answered."[152]

"But here the high priest asks if Isa Mesih is 'the Mesih, the Son of God'. He is not asking if he is the 'Son of Man' that the prophet Daniel saw in his vision. Surely it is right to condemn someone who claims to be the Son of God," commented Jamshed.

"We have to understand that the Jews also used the term 'Son of God' with a political meaning—as a title for the Mesih, the expected king. About a thousand years before Isa Mesih, God had said to the prophet Davud: 'When your days are over and you go to be with your ancestors, I will raise up your offspring to succeed you, one of your own sons, and I will establish his kingdom. He is the one who will build a house for me, and I will establish his throne forever. I will be his father, and he will be my son. I will never take my love away from him, as I took it away from your predecessor. I will set him over my house and my kingdom forever; his throne will be established forever.'[153] Jamshed, who do you think this prophecy refers to?"

"When it says that 'his throne will be established forever' it sounds like the prophecy that the prophet Daniel saw about the 'son of man.'"

"Exactly! But in this passage God says 'he will be my son'. In the *Zabur*, the second song (psalm) also refers to the 'Anointed One' and quotes God as referring to him not only as king but also as his son. So it is not surprising that the Jews began to use the term 'Son of God' as a title for the expected Mesih—the Anointed One that they thought would save them from the Romans. That is why the high priest asked Isa Mesih if he was 'the Mesih, the Son of God'. In the same way, another man who met Isa Mesih said to him, 'Rabbi, you are the Son of God; you are the king of Israel!'"[154]

"So you mean that these are all just titles for the same person? But isn't it contradictory to say both 'son of man' and 'Son of God' if they both refer to the same person?"

"It does seem strange, doesn't it, until we look at the context. When the prophet Daniel saw 'one like a son of man', was he describing a vision of earth or of heaven?"

"From the description, it was obviously in heaven, in the presence of God."

"So there in heaven, probably what had a great impression on the prophet Daniel was the fact that the one who was given such authority and power actually had a human form! In his vision of heaven, the prophet focussed on the human attributes."

"Do you mean, then, that those who described Isa Mesih here on earth were surprised by something else?"

"Exactly! For example, when Isa Mesih died, there was something about the way he died that even made a Roman soldier, who was not a Jew, respect him. What do you think this Roman centurion said?"

"Maybe he recognised something about the holy character of Isa Mesih?"

"That's right! When the Roman soldier saw how Isa Mesih died, he cried out, 'Surely this man was God's Son!'[155] Probably he was testifying to the character of Isa Mesih, rather than using the expression in the Jewish way as a title for the Messiah."

Jamshed was quiet for a moment, then commented, "I suppose we use that kind of expression when saying something derogatory about someone, like in Russian if you want to insult someone you can say, 'сукин сын' [*sukin syn*]—'son of a bitch!' Of course, it doesn't mean that the person's mother was literally a dog but it says something about the person's character. But if, by contrast, someone were to say something very respectful and positive, if you say someone is a 'son of God', it would mean that you can see God through that person."

"You know, Jamshed, Isa Mesih once said, 'Anyone who has seen me has seen the Father'.[156] In talking with Isa Mesih and seeing his life, his miracles and his character, people realized that they were coming into an encounter with God in human form."

"So these titles tell us about the character and nature of Isa Mesih," mused Jamshed. "But if the titles 'Son of Man' and 'Son of God' also meant 'King of Israel' or 'Mesih', why didn't Isa Mesih say so plainly? Why use these other words?"

"Do you think people would have accepted him if he had said so more plainly? He demonstrated it not only by the words he said but also by his miracles. His life without sin spoke far more powerfully than any claims he made about himself. We all know that actions speak louder than words."

Jamshed was silent for a moment, then suddenly chuckled to himself and said, "You know, it makes me imagine what might happen in the future in Tibet after the present Dalai Lama dies. I guess that if the Tibetans were to think that some other person was the new Dalai Lama they would not actually use that term to speak about him because they would not want the Chinese authorities to know who he was, in case they tried to prevent this person being the new Dalai Lama. So it makes sense that during the time of the Roman occupation of Israel the Jews would do something similar, using various other terms instead of saying directly that someone was the Mesih!"

"That's an interesting comparison, Jamshed," I remarked, "but I can see what you are saying."

"Nevertheless," continued Jamshed, "in the end Isa Mesih suffered and died anyway. So what did he really end up accomplishing? Where is this kingdom of his?"

"His kingdom is not bounded by geography. He is king where people acknowledge him as king in their lives. His victory was over the powers of darkness who had held people in bondage to death. By his death, as a perfect and undeserving sacrifice, he actually paid the penalty of our sin, taking on himself the punishment that each of us deserves. By doing that, he set us free from slavery to Satan and established a new kingdom that will endure in heaven for ever. That is his eternal kingdom."

"So suffering was the way to something greater. Maybe that is like what you said about the prophet Ayoub—that his friends thought his suffering was the result of his own sin but actually it was because of the unseen spiritual confrontation with Satan."

"You are right, Jamshed: I hadn't thought of it that way before! Yes, apart from his prophecy about the coming of a Redeemer, there is another aspect of the prophet Ayoub's life which is also prophetic. As I mentioned before, often our actions speak louder than our words, and this was the case also for the prophet Ayoub. In all his many sufferings he continued to see that spiritual realities are most important of all. In this, his attitude was like that of Isa Mesih. In the *Injil* it is written:

> The Mesih suffered for you, leaving you an example, that you should follow in his steps. "He committed no sin, and no deceit was found in his mouth." When they hurled their insults at him, he did not retaliate; when he suffered, he made no threats. Instead, he entrusted himself to him who judges justly."[157]

"You say that Isa Mesih was without sin?"

"Yes. And in saying of Isa Mesih that 'he committed no sin', we have the reason why he was the only one who could become a Redeemer for us. The passage just quoted continues with the words, 'He himself bore our sins in his body on the tree, so that we might die to sins and live for righteousness; by his wounds you have been healed'.[158] If even great men of God such as the prophet Ayoub or Isa Mesih were not always treated with respect and given the dignity they deserved, why should we be entitled to such things? We need to learn the lesson which is shown in the lives of both the prophet Ayoub and of Isa Mesih—namely, that knowing God himself is far more important than receiving God's blessings."

"So again it is a question of knowing God personally, not just knowing about him."

"You are right, Jamshed. Many people want to receive God's gifts but they are not concerned about developing a personal relationship with the Giver. If they have needs, they might pray and ask God to help them out of a crisis, but they do not want to listen to what God wants to say to them. They do not want to find out God's will for their lives or to do what God is calling them to do."

"Oh yes! Many of us are like that," agreed Jamshed. "We want the gifts but do not want to know the Giver! I do, however, want to get to know him better. God is gracious. He is the Giver of all life, and all good things. Even though I have suffered, I think I am also able to thank God for the gifts he has given me in my life—such as little Munira! But I agree that, more than material possessions, family or friends, what is most important is to get to know God better for who he is."

Suddenly I realised that Jamshed was no longer talking to me but to God. He switched from Russian to Tajik so I did not understand what he was saying but later he explained to me that he had prayed to God, "God, please show yourself to me and give me the courage to do whatever you are asking me to do in my life."

UZBEKISTAN: BRINGING UP CHILDREN

Crossing the border from Tajikistan into Uzbekistan was an unusual experience. From Khujand I had to take a taxi to the border, where iron gates on both sides of a bridge separated the two countries.[159] Cars were not permitted to go through the border so I had to walk across 'no man's land' and into Uzbekistan. From that border I then had to arrange another vehicle to take me to Tashkent.

I was reminded of the first time I had crossed the border between Tajikistan and Uzbekistan, and had not even noticed that I had done so. It was in 1982, when the whole area was part of the Soviet Union. From Samarkand I had travelled to the archaeological site of the ancient city of Panjakent, where over a thousand years ago the culture of the Sogdian people flourished. Their language was of an Iranian type and Samarkand was one of their centres for trade along the Silk Road. Even today Tajik—an Iranian language, of the Indo-European language family—is commonly spoken on the streets of Samarkand.

When I moved on to Khiva, in the region of Khorezm, Turkic languages, especially Uzbek, were those which came most often to my ears. Wandering around this ancient city, I was impressed by the architecture—especially the thick city walls and a majestically tall tower in the heart of the old city—but far more important than the buildings were the people.

In a narrow back street of Khiva, I came across a group of children playing in the street. I did not intend to interfere with their game, but as I watched them a little they suddenly noticed me and gathered round me. One of them noticed my camera and asked me to take a photo of them all. It was not a request I could refuse!

Just then two adults appeared in a doorway. Seeing the stranger with their children, they invited me to come into their home. At first I was surprised to be invited in, but decided that it would be an interesting opportunity to get to know a local family.

As we sat drinking tea, the children went outside again to play in the street. I had already told my hosts, Jasur and Nargiza, that I have five children and two granddaughters but I was not expecting their response to this information. Jasur glanced across to Nargiza, who was silently pouring some more tea, then he said to me, "You have five children. How have you managed to bring them up? It's so difficult to be a parent."

"Why do you ask about this?" I asked. "Are you having particular problems?"

"We want our children to grow up leading good, honest lives, but how do you teach them to tell the truth, not to cheat, to respect other people, not to take things that do not belong to them, and so on?"

"It's not easy to bring up children," I agreed. "Parenting is one of the most difficult jobs that we have to face in our lives. Unfortunately there are no easy answers."

Then, remembering what I had said in a different context in Kazakstan, I continued, "Many parents wish they knew some quick and simple 'magic formula' which would make their children into perfect human beings! But nobody has yet discovered such a 'magic formula'!"

"So how did you bring up your five children?"

"With lots of mistakes! But we did have someone who could teach us what parenting is supposed to be like."

"Who was that?"

"The One who invented parenting in the first place! I mean God: do you think God intended parenting to be so difficult? When God created the first man and woman he commanded them to 'be fruitful and increase in number; fill the earth and subdue it'.[160] If God created us with the possibility of having children and told the first people to populate the earth, surely he should also have given us some kind of guidance about the best ways to bring up children in a godly manner?"

"I had thought the same once," remarked Jasur. "So I looked in the Qur'an but could find hardly anything about bringing up children! I found one passage about the inheritance of property which says that boys are to receive twice as much as girls.[161] There was another passage that says that we should not kill our children.[162] The most positive teaching about children in the Qur'an is a verse which says that wealth and children are an adornment of the life of this world.[163]"

"Do you know what the prophets Suleiman and Davud wrote about children?" I asked.

"No, what did they say?"

"The prophet Suleiman wrote:

> Sons are a heritage from the LORD,
> children a reward from him.

> Like arrows in the hands of a warrior
> are sons born in one's youth.

> Blessed is the man
> whose quiver is full of them.
> They will not be put to shame
> when they contend with their enemies in the gate.[164]

The prophet Davud also wrote in the *Zabur*:

> As a father has compassion on his children,
> so the LORD has compassion on those who fear him.[165]

The prophet Davud compares the relationship between us and our children with that between God and us. God treats us like his children."

"But you can't say that God has children," interjected Jasur, obviously thinking along the same lines as Ali, whom I had met in Xinjiang.

"Do you know what is written in the Holy Book about the first man, Adam?" I replied. "There is a genealogy going back to Adam, who is then described as 'Adam, the son of God'.[166] It hardly needs to be said that this expression does not mean that Adam was God's son in a biological sense, like that of human parents. The *Taurat* describes how God created Adam 'from the dust of the ground' and breathed the breath of life into him so that Adam became a living being.[167] However, the Holy Books say that God cares for human beings, his creation, in the same way as a parent cares for a child. This is not surprising, because we are created by God and he is, in effect, the ancestor of us all."

"But Adam was a prophet, and the first human being so of course he had a special relationship with God," commented Jasur.

"Other prophets also speak in the same way of God as the father of all mankind, including you and me," I replied, "For example, the prophet Malachi said:

Have we not all one Father? Did not one God create us?[168]

Likewise, the prophet Isaiah spoke of human beings as being like God's rebellious children:

The LORD has spoken: 'I reared children and brought them up, but they have rebelled against me...'[169]

God treats us like his children in love—but at times he also has to discipline us like a Father."

"Discipline us? Yes, our children certainly need discipline!" agreed Jasur, "But how does God discipline us?"

"The prophet Suleiman wrote:

My son, do not despise the Lord's discipline,
and do not resent his rebuke,
because the Lord disciplines those he loves,
as a father the son he delights in.'[170]

This passage is also quoted in the *Injil*, which describes it as 'a word of encouragement that addresses you as sons' and goes on to say:

Endure hardship as discipline; God is treating you as sons. For what son is not disciplined by his father? If you are not disciplined (and everyone undergoes discipline), then you are illegitimate children and not true sons. Moreover, we have all had human fathers who disciplined us and we respected them for it. How much more should we submit

to the Father of our spirits and live! Our fathers disciplined us for a little while as they thought best; but God
disciplines us for our good, that we may share in his holiness. No discipline seems pleasant at the time, but painful.
Later on, however, it produces a harvest of righteousness
and peace for those who have been trained by it.[171]"

Nargiza, who had been listening intently to the conversation, broke in with a question. "So you are saying that
hardships in life can be a kind of discipline or training from
God? Is it like the times when I tell my children that they
cannot have sweets because I want them to have proper food
instead?"

"That's a good illustration," I replied. "From the beginning, when God created Adam and Eve, he wanted human
beings to enjoy a good and close friendship with God. God
intended us to have with him the same kind of good quality
time which parents want to have with their children. In the
Garden of Eden, Adam and Eve at first enjoyed a very close
relationship with God because there was no sin separating
them from fellowship with God. That's really the kind of
relationship which a parent would also like to have with a
child."

"Ideally, yes, but it doesn't happen that way," commented
Nargiza. "But, in any case, we can't see God so how can you
compare the relationship with God with that which we have
with our children?"

"Even if you are physically with your children and can see
them, does that mean that your relationship is close? A lot of
it depends on the quality of our communication. This morning I was so glad that I could chat on the phone with my wife
and our two youngest children in China. I was not with them

physically but we were able to talk about things together. It is the quality of the relationship which is important."

"Maybe that's part of our problem: the children come home from school and watch TV or play electronic games and we don't really get to talk with them apart from fairly superficial things."

I was reminded of some of the people I had already met on my journey. I wondered how many of us treat God in the same way—just saying the usual words but without real, meaningful communication. My thoughts were interrupted by Nargiza's next question.

"You said that God treats us like his children, even disciplining us—but why does he do that? Why does God allow these difficulties in our lives?"

"But you as a good parent also have to set boundaries on your children's activities, don't you?" I replied. "You know what would hurt a child. You don't want your child to touch a hot stove or to wander alone into a busy main road where he might be hit by a car. In the same way, God put limits on what Adam and Eve were allowed to do. When they disobeyed God's command, they needed to face the consequences. You are loving parents and I know you do not like to punish your children but you still recognise that sometimes you need to do so, for your child to learn what is best."

"Yes, I suppose so," agreed Nargiza.

"Often this process of education involves *trust*," I continued. "Your children may not understand fully why they have to be careful when crossing a busy road but they have to trust you when you tell them it is safe to cross. To develop such trust, obedience is necessary: the child has to learn to obey what you say."

"That's fair enough when our children were smaller, but now they are at school and becoming teenagers, they don't just want a set of rules," responded Jasur.

"Exactly—however much we as parents love our newborn babies, we would not want them to remain always as just infants. We look forward to the day when our children will converse with us and do things together with us. We want to have children who will eventually become responsible adults themselves. In this process, the children have to learn for themselves what is right and what is wrong."

"So how do they do that?" queried Jasur, "How do they learn to become responsible and to decide for themselves what is right and wrong? That's the problem we're facing nowadays."

"As infants and younger children they had to trust their parents, but over time they begin to recognise certain principles. They learn to apply those principles in new situations. God teaches us in the same way. In the Holy Books he has given us good laws and principles. However, we also need to apply those principles to new situations. For example, through the prophet Musa, and others, God said, 'Do not steal'.[172] Nowadays we need to apply this principle also to the relationships between rich countries and poor countries, to employers and employees, or to customers and businesses."

"But how do principles differ from rules? Isn't it more or less the same?"

"It is rather like driving a car. When we learn to drive, we are taught the rules of the road and how to operate the controls of the car. However, once we pass our driving test and we drive along the road by ourselves we have to apply those principles to new and unexpected situations. That is how God teaches us. He gives us the principles so we can live in the right way and not have accidents. If we disregard God's principles it can lead to disaster, just as disasters happen if we do not obey the rules of the road."

"But how does that apply to bringing up children?"

"It is just the same with bringing up children. Parents can teach their children the basic rules of right and wrong but the children themselves have to apply those rules to the situations they face in everyday life. At school or other places they can be influenced in the wrong way by other people, so they need to know how to distinguish for themselves between right and wrong. Parents cannot know the details of each and every situation which their children will face, but they can teach their children the right moral guidelines so that the children can apply those principles in daily life."

"So you're saying it's just a question of teaching some basic principles?"

"No, it's not simply that. You remember what I said at the beginning about knowing the One who teaches us how to be good parents?"

"You said something about having someone who could teach us what parenting is supposed to be like."

"That's exactly it—it's a relationship, not simply a matter of saying the right words or doing the right things. God has given us further help in making our decisions. He has created each human being with a conscience. If we learn to listen to the inner voice of our conscience it can often tell

113

us what is right and what is wrong. The *Injil* tells us: 'whenever the Gentiles, who do not have the law, do by nature the things required by the law, these who do not have the law are a law to themselves. They show that the work of the law is written in their hearts, as their conscience bears witness and their conflicting thoughts accuse or else defend them.'[173] Unfortunately, however, our consciences can sometimes become dulled. It becomes dulled when we ignore the voice of conscience and act against it. The voice of our consciences can also be stifled by the bad examples of those around us, including our own parents and friends. We think, 'Others do it, so it must be all right'. If at first we felt uncomfortable about it, in time we no longer hear the cry of our conscience."

"So are you saying that the voice of our conscience is actually the voice of God?"

"Often I think it probably is, yes, but there is much more to it than that. Besides our conscience—and, I think, far more importantly—God has given us another Counsellor, who will be with us for ever and will teach us the right way to go. God is like a good parent who is still available and willing to give advice and guidance when the children face difficult decisions. Adult children have to ask for that guidance and advice and be willing to receive it. In the same way, we have to invite God's Counsellor to come to us and help us in our lives."

"What kind of Counsellor are you talking about?"

"God is like a parent who wants to develop good character in his children. That is why the Holy Book says, 'we also rejoice in our sufferings, because we know that suffering produces perseverance; perseverance, character; and character, hope. And hope does not disappoint us, because God has poured out his love into our hearts by the Holy Spirit, whom he has given us.'"[174]

114

"Who is this Holy Spirit? Is this the Counsellor you mean?"

"Yes. God himself comes to us through his Holy Spirit. We have to be willing to receive God's Holy Spirit and let the Spirit of God teach us the true way. He is the Spirit of Truth who can restore our dulled consciences and teach us what is good and right. The Holy Spirit can come to us and give us a new spirit."

"Hmm... If I understand you correctly, is it a bit like my teaching my son to play the *dombra*? It's not enough just to give him a book, or even to show him how to put his fingers in the right places to make the chords, but he learns best when we both play together and I can be playing alongside him."

"That's a good way of thinking about it—and is rather like what I was saying about becoming God's children. When the Holy Spirit comes, it is what the *Injil* refers to as our 'adoption' as sons of God.[175] It is written: 'All who are led by the Spirit of God are the sons of God. For you did not receive the spirit of slavery leading again to fear, but you received the Spirit of adoption, by whom we cry, "Abba, Father." The Spirit himself bears witness to our spirit that we are God's children. And if children, then heirs (namely, heirs of God and also fellow heirs with the Mesih)–if indeed we suffer with him so we may also be glorified with him.'[176] God is not a parent who says 'do this, do that' without enabling us to have the resources to do what he intends. That power comes through the Holy Spirit of God living in us."

"So just as we want our children to be honest, you are saying that God wants the same for us?"

"Exactly! We as parents want to develop integrity of character and maturity in our children. God desires the same for his children. The difference is that, through his Holy Spirit, God gives us the power to do it—to live in a right and true way."

"So what difference does the Holy Spirit make in our lives?"

"God's Holy Spirit living in us gives us the power to live as God intends, to become refined and purified in our souls. In the *Injil* it is written:

> Live by the Spirit, and you will not gratify the desires of the sinful nature. For the sinful nature desires what is contrary to the Spirit, and the Spirit what is contrary to the sinful nature. They are in conflict with each other, so that you do not do what you want. But if you are led by the Spirit, you are not under law.
>
> The acts of the sinful nature are obvious: sexual immorality, impurity and debauchery; idolatry and witchcraft; hatred, discord, jealousy, fits of rage, selfish ambition, dissensions, factions and envy; drunkenness, orgies, and the like. I warn you, as I did before, that those who live like this will not inherit the kingdom of God.
>
> But the fruit of the Spirit is love, joy, peace, patience, kindness, goodness, faithfulness, gentleness and self-control. Against such things there is no law. Those who belong to Isa Mesih have crucified the sinful nature with its passions and desires. Since we live by the Spirit, let us keep in step with the Spirit."[177]

"So how does the Holy Spirit also become our Counsellor?"

"This is the Holy Spirit whose presence with us as a Counsellor was promised by Isa Mesih, when he said:

'I tell you the truth: It is for your good that I am going away. Unless I go away, the Counsellor will not come to you; but if I go, I will send him to you. When he comes, he will convict the world of guilt in regard to sin and right-eousness and judgment: in regard to sin, because men do not believe in me; in regard to righteousness, because I am going to the Father, where you can see me no longer; and in regard to judgment, because the prince of this world now stands condemned. I have much more to say to you, more than you can now bear. But when he, the Spirit of truth, comes, he will guide you into all truth. He will not speak on his own; he will speak only what he hears, and he will tell you what is yet to come. He will bring glory to me by taking from what is mine and making it known to you. All that belongs to the Father is mine. That is why I said the Spirit will take from what is mine and make it known to you.'"[178]

"You mean that the Holy Spirit communicates to us from God? So, if God is wise, then through his Holy Spirit he can share something of his wisdom with us? We certainly need wisdom to know what to do as parents!" commented Jasur.

"Yes. The Holy Spirit is our Counsellor who lives in us and is with us all the time. He does what no human parent can do. God, the wise parent, has provided his Holy Spirit to instruct us and to lead us into a close fellowship with God. God is not a parent who has created us and abandoned us without giving us any directions in how to be parents ourselves. He disciplines us as his children, just as he even disciplined the prophets. However, he also gives us his Holy Spirit to live in us so that we can hear the voice of God and know how to live as God intends. This is the secret of real parenting."

TURKMENISTAN: CARPETS

In the living room at Guncha's home, a long loom had been set up, on which her mother was weaving a traditional style of carpet. Their family had been involved in weaving carpets for several generations and they proudly showed me examples of some of the designs which had been created by Guncha's father. They had photographs of other carpets which had been sold to others, including one which had been specially commissioned by a well-known politician depicting his face on the carpet. Guncha, their daughter, now teaches at the university and we had first met in 1990 at an academic conference at the Al-Faraby Kazak State University in Almaty. Now, a few years later, I had the opportunity to visit Turkmenistan so we had met up once again.

I admired the diligence and skill of Guncha's mother as she wove the carpet.

"It is truly a beautiful work of art," I commented to Guncha.

"Yes, my mother has been weaving carpets all her life."

Turkmenistan is famous for its carpets, with each tribe having its own distinctive motifs and patterns. As I watched the carpet slowly grow, row by row, my thoughts began to turn to the values which are expressed in the making of such carpets.

"Certainly it involves a lot of hard work!" I remarked.

"Yes, it takes a long time to produce such a carpet," agreed Guncha.

"That shows how hard-working you Turkmen people are!" I agreed.

"Really? I'd never thought of us as especially hard working!" remarked Guncha. "When I was at school some people used to look down on Turkmen culture, saying we were 'primitive aborigines' so at that time I didn't really think there was very much positive in my culture."

"Those people are wrong!" I exclaimed. "You Turkmen have many features of your culture which we can greatly respect, and from which we can learn."

"What can you learn from us?" asked Guncha, in surprise.

"For example, when your grandmother came into the room, what did we do? We stood up to greet her, as a sign of respect. In the *Taurat*, it is written 'Rise in the presence of the aged, show respect for the elderly and revere your God'.[179] Unfortunately, many people in Europe and elsewhere have forgotten such customs, so in this way we can learn from you because your customs are closer than ours to God's standards."

"I never thought that Irish people could learn anything from our culture!" exclaimed Guncha. "What else is there in our culture that is positive and good?"

I glanced at her mother weaving the carpet, then said, "Look at your mother's patience in weaving that carpet. Your carpets themselves express some of your traditional values, like hard work and patience."

"Surely your people are also hard working and patient too?"

"Some are; some aren't—just as I suppose is also true of any nationality! However, I don't think many Irish people would have the kind of patience that it takes to make such a fine carpet. Your mother's patience in making that carpet shows me something of a fine quality which the prophet Suleiman praised and encouraged us to have."

"What did the prophet Suleiman say about patience?"

"He wrote many proverbs, several of which talk about patience. For example:

> A patient man has great understanding,
> but a quick-tempered man displays folly.[180]

> A man's wisdom gives him patience;
> it is to his glory to overlook an offence.[181]

> Through patience a ruler can be persuaded,
> and a gentle tongue can break a bone."[182]

"It sounds like I ought to read some of the prophet Suleiman's proverbs!" remarked Guncha, "So what else did he write?"

"He also wrote about other values which you Turkmen express through your carpets, such as the importance of working diligently. On that topic, he wrote:

> Lazy hands make a man poor,
> but diligent hands bring wealth.

> He who gathers crops in summer is a wise son,
> but he who sleeps during harvest is a disgraceful son.[183]

> He who works his land will have abundant food,
> but he who chases fantasies lacks judgement.[184]

Go to the ant, you sluggard;
consider its ways and be wise!
It has no commander,
no overseer or ruler,
yet it stores its provisions in summer
and gathers its food at harvest.

How long will you lie there, you sluggard?
When will you get up from your sleep?
A little sleep, a little slumber,
a little folding of the hands to rest—
and poverty will come on you like a bandit,
and scarcity like an armed man."[185]

"Some of us Turkmen could learn a lesson or two from the prophet Suleiman!" remarked Guncha.

"And a lot of Irish and other people too!" I added.

"You know, I had never thought before about the values which go into the making of our carpets," continued Guncha. "Are there any other things the carpets express?"

"I suppose you could say that they even express honesty, because if one makes a mistake it is obvious and is impossible to hide!"

Guncha chuckled. "Yes, I guess you're right! That's why we work hard because we don't want to make a mistake! I suppose the prophet Suleiman must have had a lot to write about honesty too?"

"Quite a lot. Do you want to hear some examples?"

"Yes, please."

"Truthful lips endure for ever,
but a lying tongue lasts only a moment.[186]

> A truthful witness saves lives,
> but a false witness is deceitful.[187]

> The Lord detests lying lips,
> but he delights in men who are truthful.[188]

> Kings take pleasure in honest lips;
> they value a man who speaks the truth.[189]"

"I see a parallel there between the Lord, who detests lying lips, and kings, who take pleasure in honest lips," remarked Guncha.

"I am sure you are right: If kings take pleasure in honest lips, how much more does God himself—who is the King of kings!"

"What else do our carpets show us about the good qualities in our culture?"

"The most obvious one we haven't even mentioned yet—creativity."

"You are right, to make a carpet does involve considerable creativity. It has to be designed very carefully."

"Where do you think people's creativity comes from?"

"I don't know. It's inside them, part of their nature, I suppose."

"All of us have the potential to be creative in very different ways. Our human creativity comes from the Creator of all, who made us. Let me tell you what the *Taurat* says about how God made mankind. It is written:

> God said, "Let us make man in our own image, in our likeness, and let them rule over the fish of the sea and the

birds of the air, over the livestock, over all the earth, and over all the creatures that move along the ground.'[190]

Man is created in the image of the Creator. That is why we can be creative. That is why we delight in the creativity of this kind of a carpet."

"But mankind cannot be made in the image of God! God is so different from us, and so great! You cannot say that we are like God!"

"You are right that we are very different from God. God cannot be compared with anything or anyone we are familiar with because all of these are created things and God is so much greater. However, we can understand more what these verses say if we compare them with a passage in the *Taurat* just a few chapters later. There it is written:

> When God created man, he made him in the likeness of God. He created them male and female; at the time they were created, he blessed them and called them "man". When Adam had lived 130 years, he had a son in his own likeness, in his own image; and he named him Seth.[191]

In other words, just as a son reflects some of his father's qualities, so mankind also reflects some of the qualities of God, who created mankind. One of those qualities is creativity."

"I had never thought of it that way before."

"The *Taurat* also teaches that God can give special gifts of creativity to his people in order to carry out God's purposes. For example, God said to the prophet Musa:

> See, the LORD has chosen Bezalel son of Uri, the son of Hur, of the tribe of Judah, and he has filled him with the Spirit of God, with skill, ability and knowledge in all kinds

of crafts—to make artistic designs for work in gold, silver and bronze, to cut and set stones, to work in wood and to engage in all kinds of artistic craftsmanship. And he has given both him and Oholiab son Ahisamach, of the tribe of Dan, the ability to teach others. He has filled them with skill to do all kinds of work as craftsmen, designers, embroiderers in blue, purple and scarlet yarn and fine linen, and weavers—all of them master craftsmen and designers."[192]

"So if God has made us with creativity, what is the purpose of our creativity?" asked Guncha.

"To do the works God desires for us!" I replied, then quoted the words of the *Injil*, where it is written:

> Do your best to present yourself to God as one approved, a workman who does not need to be ashamed and who correctly handles the word of truth.[193]

Guncha was quiet for a while as she looked with fresh eyes at the carpet which her mother was weaving. After a while, she said,

"Why have I never heard any of our teachers tell us that we can be creative because that expresses what God puts into us? Does that apply to women as well as men?"

"It definitely does! When God created mankind in the image of God it is explicitly stated that 'he created them male and female'. God values the creativity of your mother and of yourself just as much as that of your father or husband."

"Have any other prophets shown us God's creativity too?"

"The perfect example of all these traditional values of your people is Isa Mesih. In terms of creativity, he cannot be surpassed because it is written of him:

He is the image of the invisible God, the firstborn over all creation. For by him all things were created: things in heaven and on earth, visible and invisible, whether thrones or powers or rulers or authorities; all things were created by him and for him. He is before all things, and in him all things hold together.[194]

Another passage about Isa Mesih states:

In the beginning was the Word, and the Word was with God, and the Word was God. He was with God in the beginning. Through him all things were made; without him nothing was made that has been made."[195]

"Isa Mesih was the Word of God?" exclaimed Guncha. "I have heard devout Muslims refer to Isa Mesih as the 'Word of Allah'. Is that how he has power to create?"

"In the beginning God spoke out words and everything was created. However, Isa Mesih so perfectly reflects the image of God the Creator, that it was through him that God created us. It is written:

We are God's workmanship, created in Isa Mesih to do good works, which God prepared in advance for us to do."[196]

"I had never understood this title of Isa Mesih before. Now it makes sense to me."

Guncha's mother had stopped her weaving and was listening to our conversation. Now she asked a question.

"You said that God wants us to work hard and be patient. What kind of work did Isa Mesih do?"

"The *Injil* says 'he went around doing good and healing all who were under the power of the devil, because God was with him'.[197] He spoke of his miracles as his 'works' but he had a far greater work to do than perform miracles. His greatest work was to accomplish our salvation by taking on himself the punishment which we deserve."

"Yes," interjected Guncha. "The Qur'an also says that Isa Mesih performed great miracles. Doesn't it also say that he could give life to the dead or give life to that which was without life?"[198]

"God created mankind and breathed into Adam the breath of life so he could live," I responded, "and you are right in saying that Isa Mesih could restore the dead to life. However, when people asked him, 'What must we do to do the works God requires?' Isa Mesih answered, 'The work of God is this: to believe in the one he has sent.'"[199]

"And was he as patient in performing his work as we Turkmen are?" queried Guncha's mother.

"Isa Mesih did show great patience, even in suffering. In fact, those who falsely accused him could not understand why he remained silent. He also endured patiently many beatings, taunts, mockery, being spat on, and so on, before being nailed to the cross. I think his example of patience was actually a fulfilment of a prophecy made about him centuries previously, when the prophet Isaiah wrote about Isa Mesih:

> He was oppressed and afflicted,
> yet he did not open his mouth;
> he was led like a lamb to the slaughter,
> and as a sheep before her shearers is silent,
> so he did not open his mouth.[200]"

"I heard that he died a horrible death on a cross," commented Guncha.

127

My eyes glanced down to the carpet beneath our feet and I noticed on the corner of it a design which looked rather like three crosses on a hill. It reminded me of the way in which Isa Mesih had been put to death on a cross on a hill with two others next to him, one on each side.

"Look at this motif in your carpet!" I said, "It looks rather like that hill with the three crosses on where Isa Mesih was put to death!" I then read the words from the *Injil*:

> Two other men, both criminals, were also led out with him to be executed. When they came to the place called The Skull, there they crucified him, along with the criminals—one on his right, the other on his left. Isa said, "Father, forgive them, for they do not know what they are doing".[201]

"I had never thought of that motif as anything to do with Isa Mesih," remarked Guncha, "but there it is, right under our feet!"

"Our ancestors loved Isa Mesih," interjected her mother, "and probably that's why even today some Turkmen people say to one another, 'May God go alongside you."

"Yes, there is an expression like that in Turkmen," explained Guncha. "But actually it is more literally something like 'May God be half of you'! In Turkmen it is '*Khudai yar bolsun*' or '*Khudai yaryn bolsun*'. We use it when we want to wish someone well in a venture, like starting a new business, or if they have something important to do."

"That sounds like a wonderful blessing," I replied, "May God go alongside you too."

TURKMENISTAN: KALYM

One of Guncha's friends is a medical doctor named Kei-yik. At her request, I had brought with me a specialist medical reference book in English for her. As a result, I ended up not only being introduced to Keiyik, and her husband and child, but also her parents and her younger sisters. One day I was invited for a meal at the home of the doctor's parents, Gurban and Maral.

We were seated on the floor, some of us on cushions and others just on the carpet with its deep pile and rich, colourful pattern. Gurban was next to me, just round a corner of the rug. In the other direction were seated his eldest daughter Keiyik and her husband, with their one-year old son on his mother's knee. Gurban's wife and his three other daughters kept coming in and out, sometimes sitting to eat with us but often disappearing into the kitchen to prepare food which they laid out on a cloth spread out on top of the carpet.

Our conversation touched on many topics, mainly to do with life in Turkmenistan and in Ireland. Gurban seemed to think that Europe must be a kind of paradise—an illusion which seemed to be hard to shake off, despite my telling him about the problems of unemployment, crime and so on. Gurban dismissed these problems with the remark, "All those things we have here in Turkmenistan too—but I still think that life in Ireland must be better."

"But the quality of social relationships is not as good as it is here in Turkmenistan," I observed. "For example, you have your family all around you, with your son-in-law coming with your daughter and their child to visit you often, whereas in the cities of Europe such kinds of family gatherings don't happen so often in many families. I notice that here in Ashgabat, and in other parts of Central Asia—even in Russia—people may often call in to visit their neighbours or relatives, and maybe sit and chat around the kitchen table, far more frequently than happens in London, for example, or even in Belfast or Dublin. Here you put far more value on social relationships and friendships. I think that is very important. Very often in Europe people are actually lonely and families are falling apart more than they are here."

Gurban decided that it was time to raise another topic.

"So why don't you get a Turkmen wife, then?" he suddenly asked.

I was rather taken aback by the question because Gurban knew that I have a wife and five children. I glanced around the room. Gurban's beautiful youngest daughter, who, I guessed, was probably in her late teens, was just then bringing a dish into the room. Hearing her father's question, her face turned crimson. Averting her eyes, she quickly put down the plate and disappeared into the kitchen.

"I already have a wife," I replied—even though everyone there already knew this.

"That doesn't matter: get another one!" responded Gurban. "Here in Turkmenistan you can have four wives. Come and live here and marry one of our Turkmen girls."

"But I thought that was how it used to be, not now. I heard that officially nowadays the government only recognises one wife."

"What the government says and what people do are not always the same! In practice, nobody is really going to mind if you have a second wife."

"I think my present wife would have some rather strong objections!" I replied.

Wondering how to get onto another topic, I added, "Besides which, I guess that the bride's family would still expect something equivalent to the *kalym*. When I was in Uzbekistan, I heard that an Uzbek man had to pay $500, plus various goods, to his intended wife's parents so that he could marry their daughter. In another family, elsewhere in Uzbekistan, the *kalym* some years ago was $100 plus various goods. I also heard of a man in Uzbekistan who had to pay *kalym* worth twenty cows, plus gifts to close relatives. Another man in Uzbekistan gave some gifts as *kalym* but also signed a contract that he would pay for his future wife's university education."

"You are obviously interested in the subject, then!" commented Gurban. "But, in any case, I'm a modern father, so I wouldn't want to demand *kalym* off anyone who wanted to marry one of my daughters. Nevertheless, my youngest is well-educated and very attractive, so, if I wanted, I could ask $5,000 to $10,000 as *kalym* for her."

I wanted to shift the conversation away from my own personal situation.

"So what do you think about *kalym* nowadays?" I asked. "Some say it is important to preserve these old customs, whereas others see it as an old tradition which is no longer important, as the couple's happiness does not depend on it. What do you think?"

Gurban was not going to be put off so easily.

"I think there is a much deeper question," he replied, "because the more important question is 'Who will be my husband?' or 'Who will be my wife?'. These are the questions which every young person asks at some time. Many parents also ask themselves, 'Whom should I find as a good wife for my son?' or 'Who would be a good husband for my daughter?'—as these are among the most important decisions we have to make in our lives. Questions like *kalym* are just the secondary details."

"You are right," I replied, "so that is why we need wisdom. One should not rush into a marriage which might turn out to be a disaster—so we need wisdom to know the right person for us to marry. However, where do we get wisdom from? I am sure you know that the source of wisdom is God. The prophet Suleiman wrote:

> Wisdom is more precious than rubies,
> and nothing you desire can compare with her."[202]

"Ah, but how do we get wisdom?" responded Gurban, "We have to be practical about these things!"

"The answer is given in another of God's holy books, where it is written:

> If any of you lacks wisdom, he should ask God, who gives generously without finding fault, and it will be given to him. But when he asks he must believe and not doubt, because he who doubts is like a wave of the sea, blown and tossed by the wind. That man should not think he will

receive anything from the Lord; he is a double-minded man, unstable in all he does.[203]

To receive wisdom from God we must first of all be willing to listen to God and to allow him to show us the way of truth. The prophet Suleiman also wrote:

> The fear of the Lord is the beginning of wisdom,
> and knowledge of the Holy One is understanding."[204]

"But a wise man also needs to have a wife, as well as wisdom!" retorted Gurban.

"Yes, but a wise man also knows that the wife God chooses for him is the perfect wife for him!"

"I know you like to quote the prophet Suleiman. Actually, I have been reading his proverbs too and I found one that I like:

> He who finds a wife finds what is good
> and receives favour from the Lord."[205]

"Yes, that is right—because God is the Creator of all and in that way is also the father of all. You, as a good father, want your daughter to have a good husband, and in the same way God wants each of us to have the wife or husband who is most suitable for us. That is why Isa Mesih said, 'Do not worry, saying, "What shall we eat?" or "What shall we drink?" or "What shall we wear?" For the pagans run after all these things, and your heavenly Father knows that you need them. But seek first his kingdom and his righteousness, and all these things will be given to you as well.'"[206]

"I can accept that God can give us food and drink—but how does he give us a wife?"

"Just as Turkmen parents in the past used to arrange their children's marriages, so also our heavenly Father—who provides for our daily needs of food and shelter—will also provide the suitable helper for each of his children. Do you know how the prophet Ibrahim found a wife for his son Isaak?"

"No. I've read the prophet Suleiman's proverbs but I did not see anything there about the prophet Ibrahim."

"The story is in the *Taurat*, not in the proverbs of Suleiman. Would you like me to tell you the story?"

"We Turkmen always like to hear stories!"

"The prophet Ibrahim was a very old man," I began, "far older than you or me! In his old age, God had given the prophet a son. As a good parent, the prophet wanted to make sure that his son had a good wife. However, he did not want his son to marry a woman who worshipped false gods or idols, because he knew that a faith shared by both a man and his wife is very important in any marriage. So he said to his servant:

> 'I want you to swear by the Lord, the God of heaven and the God of earth, that you will not get a wife for my son from the daughters of the Canaanites, among whom I am living, but will go to my country and my own relatives and get a wife for my son Isaak.'[207]

Taking with him ten camels and many gifts, the prophet's servant went on a long journey to the town where the prophet Ibrahim's relatives lived. There he prayed for God to guide him.

He prayed, 'O Lord, God of my master Ibrahim, give me success today, and show kindness to my master Ibrahim. See, I am standing beside this spring, and the daughters of the townspeople are coming out to draw water. May it be that when I say to a girl, "Please let down your jar that I may have a drink," and she says, "Drink, and I'll water your camels too"—let her be the one you have chosen for your servant Isaak. By this I will know that you have shown kindness to my master.' Before he had finished praying, Rebekah came out with a jar on her shoulder.'[208]

The servant hurried to meet her and said, 'Please give me a little water from your jar.'

'Drink, my lord,' she said, and quickly lowered the jar to her hands and gave him a drink. After she had given him a drink, she said, 'I'll draw water for your camels too, until they have finished drinking.' So she quickly emptied her jar into the trough, ran back to the well to draw more water, and drew enough for all his camels.[209]

This was the first sign that God intended this girl as a bride for Isaak. A second sign became clear when the servant found out that Rebekah was of the same clan as the prophet Ibrahim: 'She was the daughter of Bethuel son of Milcah, who was the wife of Ibrahim's brother Nahor. The girl was very beautiful, a virgin; no man had ever lain with her.'[210]

As Isaak had been born to Ibrahim in his old age, the prophet's brother's son's daughter was the nearest eligible young lady in the male line of descent. God had chosen the most suitable bride of all!

However, we need to be willing to do God's will. Rebekah had not met Isaak but she was willing to follow the signs which God had given, after the servant explained why he had come.

They called Rebekah and asked her, 'Will you go with this man?'

'I will go,' she said.[211]

The prophet's servant also 'brought out gold and silver jewellery and articles of clothing and gave them to Rebekah; he also gave costly gifts to her brother and to her mother.'[212]

"Ah, so he gave the family *kalym* too—just like we Turkmen!" remarked Gurban.

"Yes! And not just like the Turkmen! It is also rather like a Karachai couple I know in the Northern Caucasus who told me that no *kalym* was paid but the parents of the groom instead gave to the bride jewellery and beautiful dresses."

"So these customs of ours are described in the *Taurat* too! So God is not against such traditions?"

"It is true that we read in the *Taurat* that the prophet Ibrahim was willing to give valuable gifts to the bride's family when he wanted to find a wife for his son. However, the prophet's grandson, Yakub, did something different. Instead of giving money or material gifts, he worked for his father-in-law for seven years so that he could marry the girl he loved. In the end he actually worked for fourteen years, as his father-in-law insisted that Yakub marry both of his daughters. This was a self-sacrificial giving of himself—and of his time and energy. This kind of sacrifice of oneself usually expresses a far deeper love than is expressed by the giving of money or other material gifts."

"I suppose that's true," agreed Gurban. "After all, our money is also in some way something we have worked for, so I suppose that it also represents our time and effort in some way. It is not so much 'buying' a bride but an expression of our energies and time."

"This is also the way in which God shows his love to us. God loves each one of us so much that he is willing to give himself completely for us. God shows his love for us in a self-sacrificial manner even greater than that of the prophet Yakub."

"Ah, but God doesn't marry, so it's not like God pays any *kalym*!"

"It is true that God does not marry, but, do you know something? In fact, God is preparing a wonderful wedding feast in heaven. And do you know who is the bride?"

"No. Who could possibly be a bride in heaven?"

"We are! God loves each of us—both men and women—and wants to welcome us into heaven with the kind of celebration that we normally consider appropriate for a wedding. However, that wedding is not without its very expensive *kalym*."

"You mean that God does pay a *kalym* too? Like the prophet Ibrahim did when his servant found a bride for his son?"

"That's right!"

"So what would God give for a *kalym*?"

"God's *kalym* is far greater than that of the prophet Ibrahim or of the prophet Yakub. God's *kalym* is very costly, involving a far greater sacrifice. God loves us so much that he gave up the One who was closest to him, the One who was perfectly pure and holy. God's *kalym* is Isa Mesih himself!"

"Isa Mesih? A person? Even a prophet? What do you mean?"

137

"It is written:

> You know that it was not with perishable things such as
> silver or gold that you were redeemed from the empty way
> of life handed down to you from your forefathers, but with
> the precious blood of Isa Mesih…[213]

God's *kalym* is motivated by a very deep love for us. God
loved us so much that he was willing to give up the One who
never sinned at all, Isa Mesih, in order to bring into heaven
those who do not deserve to live with God—that is, you and
me.

Isa Mesih said about himself:

> 'Greater love has no-one than this, that one lay down his
> life for his friends. You are my friends if you do what I
> command'.[214]

"What? Become a friend of Isa Mesih? Or a friend of
God? How is this possible?"

"Writing to those who had put their trust in Isa Mesih as
their Lord and Saviour, it is written in the *Injil*:

> …when the kindness and love of God our Saviour ap-
> peared, he saved us, not because of righteous things we
> had done, but because of his mercy. He saved us through
> the washing of rebirth and renewal by the Holy Spirit,
> whom he poured out on us generously through Isa Mesih
> our Saviour…[215]

"By his mercy?" mused Gurban. "And not because of the
good things we have done? Yes, I had heard that God is merciful. And God's *kalym* is surely much greater than that which
my parents and I gave my wife's parents when I married!"

"Your paying that *kalym* has also in some way influenced
your own relationship with your wife. In a similar way, have

you considered that God's love, expressed in his *kalym*, would also affect the relationships that we have within our own families?

It is written elsewhere in the *Injil*:

> Husbands, love your wives, just as Isa Mesih loved the church and gave himself up for her to make her holy, cleansing her by the washing with water through the word, and to present her to himself as a radiant church, without stain or wrinkle or any other blemish, but holy and blameless. In the same way, husbands ought to love their wives as their own bodies. He who loves his wife loves himself. After all, no-one ever hated his own body, but he feeds and cares for it, just as Isa Mesih does the church—for we are members of his body. 'For this reason a man will leave his father and mother and be united to his wife, and the two will become one flesh.' This is a profound mystery—but I am talking about Isa Mesih and the church. However, each one of you also must love his wife as he loves himself, and the wife must respect her husband.[216]

Human love, even that between a man and his wife, is a dim reflection of the perfect love which God has for us. A marriage can be enriched by each person knowing the love of God, which can then flow out into love for one's wife or husband. In the *Injil* it is written:

> Dear friends, let us love one another, for love comes from God. Everyone who loves has been born of God and knows God. Whoever does not love does not know God, because God is love....

> God is love. Whoever lives in love lives in God, and God in him. Love is made complete among us so that we will have confidence on the day of judgement, because in this world we are like him. There is no fear in love. But perfect love drives out fear, because fear has to do with

139

punishment. The man who fears is not made perfect in love. We love because he first loved us."[217]

"God is love? Is that what you said?" remarked Gurban, "I have never thought before that God could be love—even though I know that God is merciful. If God is love, it would of course affect the way we treat other human beings whom God loves too."

"Yes, you are right. And did you know that God has also prepared a very special helper for each one of us?"

"You mean our wives?"

"Not just a wife—or a husband! Nevertheless, God made each of us unique and he has a unique partner who is the one whom God has planned to share our lives with us. After God made the first man, Adam, 'The Lord God said, "It is not good for the man to be alone. I will make a helper suitable for him".'[218]

The special helper, whom God gave to Adam, was Eve, the first woman. However, we do not need to wait until marriage to receive another helper whom God has promised to those who love him and are willing to do his will. Isa Mesih promised to send his Holy Spirit to be a helper and Counsellor for all who love God and are willing to receive this special gift of God's presence in their lives. He said:

> 'The Counsellor, the Holy Spirit, whom the Father will send in my name, will teach you all things and will remind you of everything I have said to you. Peace I leave with you; my peace I give you. I do not give as the world gives. Do not let your hearts be troubled and do not be afraid.'[219]

"Are you saying that God's Holy Spirit is a better and closer companion even than a husband or wife?"

140

"In many ways, yes, because God himself comes to us through his Holy Spirit. Whether or not we have a wife or husband in this life, what is far more important is to have the special friendship with God which comes from his Holy Spirit living in our lives. He helps us to live in the way that is best of all. Those who are willing to receive the Holy Spirit whom Isa Mesih sends as the Helper and Comforter in this life have a far better helper than any human husband or wife. At the same time, God's plan is to make a new family of holy people, who are united by the Holy Spirit of God."

"A new family of holy people?" queried Gurban. "Is this what you meant when you said that God is preparing a wonderful wedding feast in heaven?"

"A bride has to prepare herself for her wedding, so that is why God has given us his Holy Spirit, to make us more holy now, to prepare us for eternity with God in heaven. However, those who belong to the new family of God have a special wedding prepared for them: in fact, God himself is preparing the wedding feast in heaven. All who have said 'Yes' to God's invitation are together, collectively, like the bride. They can come into heaven only because of the sacrifice which God has made in giving his special *kalym*. Now we have to get ready for that 'wedding' when Isa Mesih will take his holy people to be his 'bride' for eternity. The prophet John wrote about what would happen in that day:

> Then I saw a new heaven and a new earth, for the first heaven and the first earth had passed away, and there was no longer any sea. I saw the Holy City, the new Jerusalem, coming down out of heaven from God, prepared as a bride beautifully dressed for her husband. And I heard a loud voice from the throne saying, 'Now the dwelling of God is with men, and he will live with them. They will be his people, and God himself will be with them and will be

141

their God. He will wipe every tear from their eyes. There will be no more death or mourning or crying or pain, for the old order of things has passed away.'[220]

The prophet John went on to write:

The Spirit and the bride say, 'Come!' And let him who hears say, 'Come!' Whoever is thirsty, let him come; and whoever wishes, let him take the free gift of the water of life.[221]"

KARAKALPAKISTAN: HONOURING OUR ANCESTORS

They had finished cleaning around the tomb and removing some of the grass which had grown up there. Now all the members of the Karakalpak family squatted down next to the tomb while the grandmother opened a bag she had brought with her. In it was some *naan* bread which she passed over to her eldest son. Taking it, he broke off a piece and then passed it on to the person next to him. Each in turn took the bread, ate a little and gave the rest to the next person until it had been passed all the way round the circle and back to the grandmother. Each one ate the bread in silence, remembering the dead person and what he had meant to them. Even if in their hearts they said a prayer of some kind, they did not express it openly.

I had travelled northwards from Ashgabat and had come into the north-western part of Uzbekistan, where the Karakalpak people live. In Nukus I had found a place where I could access the Internet and while there I met a Karakalpak man named Bakhadyr. He very kindly offered to show me around a little. When he learned that I was interested in knowing more about Karakalpak culture, he invited me to go the next day with some of his relatives to visit the grave of his uncle.

Afterwards, I asked my friend Bakhadyr how he feels about his relatives who have died.

"Of course I do pray to God but I feel that the *aruak*—the spirits of our ancestors—are somehow closer to us. That is why I pray to the *aruak* more than to God. I feel that God is rather distant and not so interested in me, whereas I feel the *aruak* are closer."

His words reminded me of similar ideas I had heard in Japan. This was certainly not official Islamic teaching but it is a common attitude among Karakalpaks and Kazaks.

"You must have loved your parents and grandparents very much," I remarked.

"Oh yes—they did so much for me. They brought me up and cared for me, gave me what they could, as much as they could. I owe to them my education. They were not wealthy so they could not leave me much in the way of any material inheritance but while they were alive they did so much for me, including helping with my wedding expenses. They loved me and cared for me. I owe so much to them."

"I'm sure you do," I replied, "and it is so good that you honour and respect them so much, just as your own children obviously honour you. That is something which the prophets tell us very clearly is a great responsibility of children towards their parents."

"I thought it was just something in our Karakalpak culture," replied Bakhadyr. "I've never heard anything in the Qur'an about children respecting parents."

"I was thinking of the great prophet Musa, who wrote the *Taurat*. God gave Musa ten great commandments which were so important that God even wrote them out on stone tablets so that the Jewish people would remember these commandments. One of them says, 'Honour your father and your mother, so that you may live long in the land the Lord your God is giving you."[222]

"Did the prophet Musa say that? So if I honour my parents it means that I'll live to a good old age?"

"It might mean that, but I think it is also referring to something different. The prophet Musa was bringing the Jewish people into the land which God had promised to their ancestors. However, God said that if they did not follow God's laws in that new land, and especially if they followed other gods, then they would be destroyed or else banished from their land and no longer able to live there.[223] So I think that it is also talking about how long the whole ethnic group would be able to live in the land."

"But surely those were supposed to be God's 'chosen people'! Didn't God promise their ancestor, the prophet Ibrahim, that his descendants would live in the country he had promised to them?"[224]

"You are right. God did make that promise, and from the time of the prophet Musa onwards there have been at least some descendants of Ibrahim living there, even though for long periods of time the majority have been scattered elsewhere. However, there is far more to being a descendant of Ibrahim than mere biology."

"What do you mean?"

"Many of the descendants of Ibrahim thought that being descended from the prophet put them in a special class and was a kind of guarantee that they would be blessed. However, what was far more important than biology was whether or not they lived by the same faith as their ancestor Ibrahim. The prophet Yahya said to some of them: 'You brood of vipers!

Who warned you to flee from the coming wrath? Produce fruit in keeping with repentance. And do not think you can say to yourselves, "We have Ibrahim as our father." I tell you that out of these stones God can raise up children for Ibrahim. The axe is already at the root of the trees, and every tree that does not produce good fruit will be cut down and thrown into the fire.'"[225]

"Wow! Strong stuff!" remarked Bakhadyr.

"Isa Mesih went even further and even said that they are children of the devil!"

"Really! What did he say?"

> "I tell you the truth, everyone who sins is a slave to sin. Now a slave has no permanent place in the family, but a son belongs to it for ever. So if the Son sets you free, you will be free indeed. I know you are Ibrahim's descendants. Yet you are ready to kill me, because you have no room for my word. I am telling you what I have seen in the Father's presence, and you do what you have heard from your father."

> "Ibrahim is our father," they answered.

> "If you were Ibrahim's children," said Isa, "then you would do the things Ibrahim did. As it is, you are determined to kill me, a man who has told you the truth that I heard from God. Ibrahim did not do such things. You are doing the things your own father does."

> "We are not illegitimate children," they protested. "The only Father we have is God himself."

> Isa then said to them, "If God were your Father, you would love me, for I came from God and now am here. I have not come on my own; but he sent me. Why is my language not clear to you? Because you are unable to hear

what I say. You belong to your father, the devil, and you want to carry out your father's desire. He was a murderer from the beginning, not holding to the truth, for there is no truth in him. When he lies, he speaks his native language, for he is a liar and the father of lies."[226]

"I can understand why they should say that the prophet Ibrahim was their ancestor, but why should they call God their father too? Surely God cannot have children?"

"God is the creator of all, and in that way we can all be regarded as his children. Speaking through the prophet Isaiah, God said:

Hear, O heavens! Listen, O earth!
For the Lord has spoken:
"I reared children and brought them up,
But they have rebelled against me.
The ox knows his master,
the donkey his owner's manger,
but Israel does not know,
my people do not understand".[227]

Elsewhere the prophet Isaiah addressed God in the following way:

Look down from heaven and see
from your lofty throne, holy and glorious.
Where are your zeal and your might?
Your tenderness and compassion are withheld from us.
But you are our Father,
though Ibrahim does not know us
or Israel acknowledge us;
you, O Lord, are our Father,
our Redeemer from of old is your name.[228]

Similarly, the prophet Malachi said:

147

Have we not all one Father? Did not one God create us?
Why do we profane the covenant of our fathers by break-
ing faith with one another?[229]"

"So really God is our ultimate ancestor, then!" exclaimed
Bakhadyr. "Could you therefore say that Adam, the first man,
was in a sense God's son? Does that make us all in some way
descendants of God, through Adam?"

"You are very perceptive, Bakhadyr!" I replied, "Do you
know how the genealogy of Isa Mesih describes Adam, the
first man?"

"How?"

"Just as you said—as the son of God! It is written: 'Isa,
when he began his ministry, was about thirty years old. He
was the son (as was supposed) of Joseph, the son of Heli, the
son of Matthat, the son of Levi, the son of Melchi, ...' and so
on, through many generations, right back to the first human
beings. The genealogy ends up saying, '...the son of Enosh,
the son of Seth, the son of Adam, the son of God'!"[230]

"Interesting..." mused Bakhadyr, then commented, "You
said that the prophet Musa wrote that we have to honour
our father and mother. Doesn't that also mean honouring
our grandparents, as they are the parents of our parents,
and so on back through all our ancestors? Isn't that what we
Karakalpaks do when we remember the *aruak*?"

"You are right that we are supposed to honour our father
and mother, and, by extension, you can say that applies to all
our ancestors. But to which ancestor should go the greatest
honour? To the most recent one or to the ancestor of the
whole clan?"

"I would say that the original ancestor of the whole clan was more important."

"So who was the original ancestor of your clan?"

"Actually, I have to say that I don't know! Anyway, I suppose if we could trace it all the way back we'd end up with Adam, the first man. But you have just told me that in fact Adam was the son of God, as he was created by God...." Bakhadyr paused for a moment, thinking, then added, "... which, I suppose, means that really God is the one we should honour most of all!"

"You are right, Bakhadyr!"

"But what about the *aruak*? Shouldn't I honour my ancestors too?"

"It is right to honour your ancestors, but they should not take the place of God. People were made by God and it is idolatry to put people in the place of God. The prophet Isaiah said, 'When men tell you to consult mediums and spiritists, who whisper and mutter, should not a people inquire of their God? Why consult the dead on behalf of the living?'[231] Likewise, the prophet Musa said that we should not try to make contact with spirits of the dead: it is written, 'Do not turn to mediums or seek out spiritists, for you will be defiled by them. I am the LORD your God.'"[232]

"Defiled? Made dirty, or contaminated, by consulting the dead? Is that what you mean?"

"Yes, we become spiritually dirty if we try to make contact with spirits of the dead. That is one reason why people can become affected by 'unclean'—that is, 'dirty'—spirits."

"When we go to the mosque we wash our physical bodies but I don't know how our spirits can be made clean. However, I've heard of a number of cases of people who seem to be affected by evil spirits. Is that because they have consulted the dead?"

"It could also be from other causes, but basically it comes from some kind of sin. However, the good news is that Isa Mesih has the power to drive out the dirty spirits and to make us clean again by his Holy Spirit. Those who belong to Isa Mesih can also exercise this authority over demons in the name and authority of Isa Mesih."[233]

"Wow! So Isa Mesih can set people free from demons!"

"Yes, but they have to repent of their sin and invite God's Holy Spirit to come into their lives and replace the darkness with light."[234]

"Are there things which we do for the dead which can allow demons to come in?"

"It depends very much on the culture and the meanings attached to certain practices. For example, at the time of the prophet Musa people made cuts in their own bodies or put tattoos on them for the dead, or shaved their hair in certain ways for the dead.[235] The prophet Musa condemned such practices because the people were to be holy to God: instead, they were being defiled by honouring the dead in the wrong way."

"So how can I respect and honour my ancestors in the right way and not the wrong way? How is it possible to honour the dead without worshipping them or praying to them as if they were equal to God?"

"Essentially we have to recognise what belongs to God and not to give to the dead that which is supposed to be given to God. That could apply to food offerings too.[236] It might not be the *form* of a certain custom but instead what we have to be careful about is the *meaning* which is attached to that practice. God looks at the heart."

"Yes, God looks at the heart, but my relatives and other people look at what I do. What is important to my relatives is whether or not I go to the grave and perform the correct rituals there. They don't really seem to be bothered about what it means."

"Unfortunately, that is a very common attitude all over the world. People think that what is important is doing the right thing after a person has died—performing the customary memorial rites and so on. However, it is far more difficult to respect and care for an elderly relative while he or she is still alive."

"That's true!"

"In fact, Isa Mesih strongly criticised people who thought that by doing the customary rituals they could get out of properly honouring their parents. Even in his day there were people who used religion as an excuse for not really caring for their parents."

"Really? What did they do?"

"Can I read to you what Isa Mesih said about this?"

"Please do!"

I picked up my *Injil* and read the following words of Isa Mesih, who said:

"You have a fine way of setting aside the commands of God in order to observe your own traditions! For Musa said, 'Honour your father and your mother,' and 'Anyone who curses his father or mother must be put to death.' But you say that if a man says to his father or mother: 'Whatever help you might otherwise have received from me is *corban*' (that is, a gift devoted to God), then you no longer let him do anything for his father or mother. Thus you nullify the word of God by your tradition that you have handed down. And you do many things like that."[237]

Bakhadyr thought for a moment about this, then commented, "I suppose it is a lot easier to think that you are honouring your dead relatives if you go to the cemetery and perform a ritual at their graves, like we did today at my uncle's tomb. But only God knows what we are thinking in our hearts and whether or not we really respected and honoured that person."

Bakhadyr paused, then added, "What was that word you read, that those people used, that means that something is 'a gift devoted to God'? Was it something like 'Kurban'?"

"Isa Mesih quoted the Hebrew word '*qorban*', which means a 'gift' or 'sacrifice' offered to God. Why do you ask?"

"We have the same word! All over Central Asia we practice the festival of Kurban Bayram, the 'Sacrifice Festival', when we sacrifice a sheep. Some men even have the name Kurban as their personal name!"

"Yes, in Turkmenistan I met a man called 'Gurban', whose name is the same as 'Kurban'. In Tatarstan I have a friend called Kurbangali."

"So maybe we also need to think more deeply about the meaning of our sacrifices! As you say, God looks at the heart, so it is not the form of the ritual that is important, but the meaning!"

"I agree!"

Bakhadyr then remembered that we had been talking about visiting the graves and remembering those who had died. He wanted to ask another question: "So what forms of practices would be all right in remembering my ancestors?"

"Bakhadyr, you told me that you do not know who the ancestor of your clan was. What do you know about your grandparents or their parents?"

"I know a little, but not very much. I know where they lived and what they did for a living."

"Perhaps you could try to construct a family tree to show who was who in your family. I think that would help your children too. Then you could try to write out in a book what you do remember about each of your ancestors and maybe try to put together any photographs you have, or even newspaper cuttings or things people have written about them. In the Holy Books there are many examples of the importance of keeping family trees.[238] That is one positive way to respect and remember the dead."

"That's a good idea: I'd never thought of making a family tree," said Bakhadyr.

"You could even put it somewhere in your house which is special, a place of honour."

"Is there any other way I can remember my ancestors?"

"You might want to have some special events or celebrations at times to remember them, but at the same time to remember how much more God has done for you. God tells us to remember important things and to keep signs as reminders of them. For example, do you know what event the rainbow is supposed to remind us of?"

"I never thought of a rainbow as reminding us of something. I just think it is beautiful, although unfortunately it doesn't last very long."

"God instituted the rainbow as a sign and memorial of his covenant with the prophet Nuh. It reminds us of God's promise that never again would the earth be flooded in the same way as happened at the time of the prophet Nuh.[239] I suppose that the fact that a rainbow doesn't last might also be a reminder that the judgement of the Flood did not last for ever."

"I never knew that! Now I'll never look at a rainbow in the same way again!"

"Maybe that is another example of what I said about forms and meanings! The form of the rainbow will be unchanged but you will now see a different meaning in it!"

"But even though God is our ultimate ancestor, I still have a lot to thank my parents and grandparents for, as they did so much for me."

"Certainly—but really God is the one to thank because we bring nothing into this world and bring nothing out of it. God made all the land we live on, and the plants and animals we eat, so whatever your parents and grandparents received was really only what God had entrusted to them."

"But they still left me some property as an inheritance, even if it was not very much."

"Do you know what the inheritance is that God gives us?"

"No, I never even suspected that we would inherit anything from God!"

"In the *Injil* it is written:

Praise be to the God and Father of our Lord Isa Mesih! In his great mercy he has given us new birth into a living hope through the resurrection of Isa Mesih from the dead, and into an inheritance that can never perish, spoil or fade—kept in heaven for you, who through faith are shielded by God's power until the coming of the salvation that is ready to be revealed in the last time.[240]"

"What kind of an inheritance is that—one that 'can never perish, spoil or fade'?"

"If it is kept in heaven for us, what kind of things do you think it could be?"

"Life with God? Living with God in heaven? Something like that?"

"Yes. That's the final part of it, but we also receive a first instalment now, like a deposit."

"Now? What can we receive now?"

"Again, it is written in the *Injil*:

Having believed, you were marked in the Mesih with a seal, the promised Holy Spirit, who is a deposit guaranteeing our inheritance until the redemption of those who are God's possession."[241]

"The Holy Spirit? Who is that?"

155

"God is holy, so the Holy Spirit is the Spirit of God. Nevertheless, he can come to live in us and his presence means that we can know God in a personal way.

Again, in the *Injil* it is written:

Because you are sons, God sent the Spirit of his Son into our hearts, the Spirit who calls out, "Abba, Father." So you are no longer a slave, but a son; and since you are a son, God has made you also an heir."[242]

"Heirs of God? Wow! But I don't feel like I deserve to be an heir of God."

"As I said, God is holy. We don't deserve to live in his holy presence because all of us have become spiritually dirty in some way by our sin. There was only one rightful heir who is pure and holy. However, the one who did deserve the inheritance chose to give it up in order to share it with us."

"Really? Who is this person? What kind of rightful heir would share the inheritance with someone like me, who doesn't deserve it?"

"He is the one who is the 'heir of all things'. In the *Injil* it is written:

In the past God spoke to our forefathers through the prophets at many times and in various ways, but in these last days he has spoken to us by his Son, whom he appointed heir of all things, and through whom he made the universe."[243]

"You said that Adam was in some way God's son, as he was created by God, but I'm sure that God did not make the universe through Adam. No, the universe was made before Adam. So this must be someone else. Do you perhaps mean Isa Mesih?"

"As I said before, Bakhadyr, you are very perceptive!"

"But you also said that he gave up his right to the inheritance. How could this be?"

"It is written:

> Isa Mesih was the mediator of a new will, so that those who are called may receive the promised eternal inheritance, now that Isa Mesih has died as a ransom to set them free from the sins committed under the first will. In the case of a will, it is necessary to prove the death of the one who made it, because a will is in force only when somebody has died; it never takes effect while the one who made it is living."[244]

"You mean that, because he died, he made a way whereby we could receive the inheritance that he alone deserved?"

"That's right. He did not need to die but he allowed himself to be put to death for our sakes. He himself said:

> 'I am the good shepherd; I know my sheep and my sheep know me—just as the Father knows me and I know the Father—and I lay down my life for the sheep. I have other sheep that are not of this sheep pen. I must bring them also. They too will listen to my voice, and there shall be one flock and one shepherd. The reason the Father loves me is that I lay down my life—only to take it up again. No-one takes it from me, but I lay it down of my own accord. I have authority to lay it down and authority to take it up again. This command I received from my Father.'"[245]

"But if Isa Mesih also had authority to take back his life again, why didn't he do so?"

"That's the good news: he did! On the third day after his death he rose again from the grave. That showed that he had authority even over death itself. Therefore we too do not need to fear death, if we belong to Isa Mesih, because he has conquered death. It is because of this that we too can share with him the inheritance—that is, eternal life."

"Eternal life—that is definitely a far better inheritance than anything my human ancestors can give me."

"Certainly! And, as I said, we even have a deposit guaranteeing that inheritance—the Holy Spirit who works in our lives to make us more prepared for life in heaven."

"Can I receive the Holy Spirit?"

"Yes, you simply have to invite him to come into your life and to change you."

"But I don't know what words to say!"

"God looks at our hearts and understands what we want to say. It does not have to be a special formula. God also understands all languages so you can pray it in the Karakalpak language, which is the language of your heart. If you do not know how to pray, you can use prayers which are already in the Holy Books as a model to give you ideas but the important thing is to talk with God in sincerity."

"Could you show me a prayer I could use as a model?"

"There are many possibilities," I replied. Opening up the Holy Book, my eyes fell on the following passage—a prayer which also mentions about the inheritance promised by God to those who love him:

> We pray this in order that you may live a life worthy of the Lord and may please him in every good work, growing in the knowledge of God, being strengthened with all power according to his glorious might so that you may have great endurance and patience, and joyfully giving thanks to the

Father, who has qualified you to share in the inheritance of the saints in the kingdom of light.[246]"

"Perhaps you could base your prayer on this one in the *Injil* and make it into an invitation for God's Holy Spirit to fill you." I suggested.

Bakhadyr read through the prayer and thought about it, then began to talk to God in his own words, saying: "God, I pray that I may live a life worthy of you. I want to please you in every good work, growing in the knowledge of you and being strengthened with all power according to your glorious might. Please send me your Holy Spirit to give me that power, so that I may have great endurance and patience and may joyfully give thanks to you, heavenly Father. I want to know you better, so that by knowing you I may be qualified to share in the inheritance of the saints in the kingdom of light."

KALMYKIA: PROVERBS

When the train stopped at Astrakhan, a man got on who took the berth next to mine. There were several hours still left on my long train journey around the northern shore of the Caspian Sea. The new passenger looked as if he might be from somewhere in Mongolia or northern China and my guess was not too far wrong. I began to chat with him and learned that by nationality he was Kalmyk. His ancestors had migrated to this region of Russia about four centuries ago, coming from what is now Xinjiang in China. They were not Chinese but Western Mongols, known in China as Oirats and now in Russia known as Kalmyks.

I took the opportunity to ask Batur about the Kalmyk people and their culture. After a while, he started to talk about some of their proverbs. He told me that there is a certain genre of sayings which says something about three or four different things and then compares them—often with a little joke in the way they are compared. For example:

Three things are splendid:
Splendid is the full moon,
Splendid is a flower of the virgin steppe,
Splendid are the exhortations of parents![247]

"Another one goes like this," continued Batur:

"Four things in the world are in great quantity:
Without an archery match there are many marksmen,
Without a wrestling match there are many wrestlers,

Without opponents there are many heroes,
Without a blacksmith there are many tinsmiths."[248]

"That's fascinating!" I commented. "Are these kinds of sayings very old among your people, or have they been made up in recent times?"

"There are lots of these kinds of sayings," replied Batur, "and as far as I know they have a long history—from ancient times."

"I can well believe that," I responded. "Did you know that there were proverbs with a similar kind of structure in the Middle East some three thousand years ago?"

"No, I'd never heard that. I thought these were unique to the Kalmyks."

"The actual examples you have quoted may well be unique, but the genre—the style of saying there are three or four things which are similar—is very similar to proverbs which are written in the Bible."

"The Bible? But our people are Buddhists, not Christians!"

"These proverbs come from the Jewish scriptures, a long time before the time of Jesus Christ."

"What kinds of things are they? Tell me a few of them."

"There are three things that are too amazing for me,
four that I do not understand:

the way of an eagle in the sky,
the way of a snake on a rock,
the way of a ship on the high seas,
and the way of a man with a maiden."[249]

Batur chuckled. "No, I can't say that I understand that either!" he said, "Tell me another."

>"Four things on earth are small,
>yet they are extremely wise:

>Ants are creatures of little strength,
>yet they store up their food in the summer;

>Coneys are creatures of little power,
>yet they make their home in the crags;

>Locusts have no king,
>yet they advance together in ranks;

>A lizard can be caught with the hand,
>yet it is found in kings' palaces."[250]

"That one says four things are extremely wise. It reminds me of one we have which is also about wisdom."

"How does it go?" I asked.

>"Three things are without end:

>Endless the starry sky,
>Endless the wisdom of man,
>Endless the stupidity of man."[251]

"Do you believe that?" I enquired.

"Well, I can't say that man's wisdom is endless, but certainly his stupidity seems to know no bounds!"

"Yes, I'm sure you're right. What kinds of things did you have in mind when you said that?"

Suddenly, Batur became silent. He looked out of the window for a while. I could not see his face very well but I wondered if he seemed to be almost about to cry. Finally, he turned back towards me and said,

"The greatest stupidity I know was when my parents were sent to Siberia. It was not only my parents but all of our people—thousands of men, women and children, herded like animals into cattle trucks and sent far away from our homeland. Many of them died on the way. Many others died in Siberia. That was such a stupid waste of life—such needless cruelty."

Batur was obviously distressed by what he knew of the events, even though they had happened to his parents and not to himself. I was uncertain whether or not I should ask any more but Batur himself began to talk, as if he felt that he had to unburden himself.

"We were not traitors! None of us—or, if any, only a handful—collaborated with the Germans and betrayed our fatherland. You can't say that a whole people were guilty of treason! But that is what Stalin accused us of—helping the Germans when they had occupied our homeland for a short time during the war. It was just not fair. The Russians came and herded us all up like animals, even children who couldn't have done anything wrong. My parents were sent away into exile. They had nothing. On top of that, they told lies about us. In Siberia the local people didn't accept us because they had been told that we were being punished because we were cannibals!"

"Horrible!" I agreed. I remembered Shamil in Kazakstan, whose wife's parents had also been deported from the Caucasus region under Stalin. Not only had the Kalmyks suffered deportation but the same had happened to peoples like the Chechen, Ingush, Karachai, Balkars, Meskhetian Turks and others who had been sent to Central Asia. The Crimean

Tatars had also been deported from the Crimea and similar policies had been used for Koreans living in the Russian Far East and Finns from northern Russia, who were also deported to Central Asia, away from the sensitive border regions.

"Not just horrible," responded Batur. "It was mass murder! I was a little baby when my parents were sent to Siberia and I was lucky to have survived. My mother died, mainly because of starvation. She would try to feed me but didn't have enough for herself. That is why she didn't have enough strength to resist infection."

"That's terrible," I agreed, not knowing what else I could say. Though Batur must have been in his sixties, the pain of his childhood memories was clearly still with him.

I wondered what else I could say. Simply saying "That's terrible" did nothing to help ease the pain in Batur's heart, but no words seemed to be adequate. What else could one say?

My silence was broken by Batur himself. He reached over for the Bible from which I had been reading the Jewish proverbs and he began to turn over its pages. Finally, he asked,

"What does this book say anyway? Does it say why God would allow such a thing to happen?"

I thought for a moment, then replied, "The book is about a nomadic people, like your ancestors were. It describes how they had once been slaves in a foreign land but God rescued them from slavery. They were brought into freedom because God loved them and wanted them to have a close and genuine relationship with him. However, when they forgot about God and ignored his wisdom—that is, when they chose to live life by their own standards instead of God's standards—they ended up being deported to a foreign land."

165

"Deported? Like us Kalmyks? Did they never return to their own land?"

"Only seventy years later. Many never returned at all."

"Seventy years in exile? That's three generations! That's far longer than the thirteen years we Kalmyks were in exile."

"Yes."

"We Kalmyks lost a lot of our culture when we were in Siberia. Many of the younger generation born in exile grew up not really being able to speak Kalmyk, as they had to speak Russian all the time. Was it the same for the people you were speaking about?"

"They were Jewish people. To some extent they might have lost some of their Hebrew language because, after their return to their own land, it seems that many ordinary people often spoke the Aramaic language spoken by those around them. However, what might have been more important was that they also lost many of the superstitions and wrong beliefs and practices which they had been practising before."

"Yes, we Kalmyks also forgot a lot about Buddhist teachings while we were in exile. So did the Jewish people also lose their religion? Did they become atheists?"

"No—in fact, they rediscovered the pure faith of their ancestors. Over a thousand years before their deportation, the ancestors of the Jewish people had been nomads who worshipped just one God. It was this God who had told their ancestor to move from his homeland and to migrate westwards to the land God would show him."

"Our ancestors also migrated westwards! They too were nomads!" exclaimed Batur.

"Like your ancestors, life for the Jewish people was not easy. At one time, when there was a great famine, they migrated again and settled in Egypt, but there they were eventually forced into slavery. Nevertheless, God was faithful to his promise to their ancestors and, by means of many miracles, God saved the people from slavery and brought them into the land he had promised to give to them."

"But you said that later they were deported from there. Why was that?"

"They forgot the one true God who had rescued them from slavery and had brought them into that land. Instead of worshipping one God, the Creator of the whole universe and of everyone in the world, they began to worship many other spirits. In the end, the God of justice and truth allowed them to be deported so that they would no longer worship many spirits but would turn back to the original faith of their ancestors. For the Jewish people, the period of deportation was a refining process. "

"That's interesting. Our ancestors originally worshipped Tenger, or Tengri, the great God of Heaven. He too was a god of justice, judging people fairly. He was the One who created the universe. It sounds like our Tenger or Tengri—the Eternal Sky—was rather like the god you are telling me about."

"Do your people still worship him?"

"No—or, at least, I don't know of anyone who does. Our ancestors also worshipped some other gods, then they became Buddhists."

"How do you think Tengri feels about that?"

"What a question! I never thought about that! I suppose he would feel angry. After all, as Tengri was the one who created the universe we ought to remember him."

"Many other peoples around the world also worshipped at the beginning a great Sky God who was thought of as the creator, the one who was also good and just. There was a German professor named Wilhelm Schmidt who documented in great detail such beliefs from all around the world.[252] However, in many cases people forgot about this good and righteous god or lost their relationship with him because of something wrong they had done—so then they began to serve many other gods or evil spirits."

"I didn't know that! What I do know, however, is that many of the Turkic peoples of Central Asia began to use the word Khodai to refer to Tengri, even after Islam came in, and that they preferred that name for God. I think that in Turkey they also refer to God as Tanrı."

"What else do you know about Tengri?"

"Apparently there used to be a great ceremony once a year when everyone gathered together to make a sacrifice to Heaven and to pray for his blessing on people and their livestock. Loads of people gathered together and the Khan himself led the ceremony—not a shaman or priest or anyone like that. This went on for about one and a half thousand years, every year, until about the fourteenth century of the present era."[253]

"Fascinating! That reminds me of the ancient custom in China, which continued right until the early twentieth century, when it was the Emperor who prayed, on behalf of the Chinese people, at the Temple of Heaven for God's blessing on the Chinese people and their crops. You know, the

Chinese word for 'Heaven' is 'Tian' (天) and the Emperor prayed to 'Tian', who was also regarded as the supreme creator of all. From the earliest inscriptions onwards, there is mention of prayers to the Supreme God and Creator of all, known to the Chinese as 'Shang Di' (上帝) – 'The Lord Above'.[254] However, another name which later became commonly used for this god was 'Tian'. Tian can mean simply 'Sky' but it was also the title for the 'Lord of Heaven'.[255] I wonder whether the names 'Tengri' and 'Tian' were originally related?"

"They sound similar, don't they? And it sounds as if they meant more or less the same. My ancestors used the term Tenger or Tengri to refer not only to the sky itself but to the Lord of Heaven, just like you say the Chinese used the word 'Tian'."

Suddenly, Batur's expression changed. His eyes opened wide in surprise, and he exclaimed, "But the Chinese have always been our enemies! We Mongolians were fighting them so often over the centuries. And now we're saying that we worshipped the same God!"

"Very often the Chinese also forgot Shang Di, or Tian, and instead worshipped other spirits, just as your ancestors did. It is rather like the Arabs and the Jews who have so often been in conflict with each other, but each claims to worship the God who led their ancestor to become a nomad and to travel westwards from what is now Iraq. The Arabs refer to that nomad as the prophet Ibrahim and respect him highly."

"How terrible that now they fight over religion if they both claim to worship the same God."

"Actually, even as long ago as the fifth century AD—long before Islam appeared—Arabic-speaking Christians were calling God by the name 'Allah'.[256] Even today in the Middle

169

East, Arab Christians still use 'Allah' as the name for God. It is not a question of the name we use for God but what we mean by that name."

"What we mean by that name? What do you mean?"

"A name can mean so many things to different people. Your name, Batur, means 'hero' in your language but others would not understand what it means. In the same way, when people refer to the 'God of Heaven' they might use names like 'Tengri' or 'Tenger', or else 'Tian' or 'Shang Di', or 'Allah' or 'God' but essentially these are all titles or descriptions. Our problem is that we argue over the name without realising that the most important thing is coming into a personal relationship with God. What is more important—getting your name right or understanding properly what kind of a person you are, knowing your character and knowing you as a friend?"

"I'd much rather that people treat me as a friend, even if—like you—they still can't pronounce my name properly!"

"Fair enough! Don't you think God feels the same? If you think about it, surely God is so much greater than any human name. We have to use our tongues and mouths to pronounce any name but do you think God is much greater than those sounds?"

"I had not thought of it that way before."

"I think that is why God did not tell his name when a great prophet asked what he should call him."

"Really?"

"Yes, the prophet whom the Arabs call 'Musa' and the Jews call 'Moshe' was in the desert looking after sheep—I suppose, rather like many of your Kalmyk ancestors. He then heard God speaking to him and telling him to go to set free his people who had been enslaved in Egypt.

Then the prophet 'said to God, "Suppose I go to the Israelites and say to them, 'The God of your fathers has sent me to you,' and they ask me, 'What is his name?' Then what shall I tell them?"

> God said to Musa, 'I AM WHO I AM. This is what you are to say to the Israelites: "I AM has sent me to you."'

> God also said to Musa, 'Say to the Israelites, "The LORD, the God of your fathers—the God of Ibrahim, the God of Isaak and the God of Yakub—has sent me to you." This is my name for ever, the name by which I am to be remembered from generation to generation."'[257]

"I like that title—'The God of your fathers'—it seems to be so much easier to remember than any name!"

"Yes, this is the God who was there at the very beginning. God did not say he was the god of the present generation's parents or grandparents, who had often forgotten the original god worshipped by their ancestors. Instead, God went back to those ancestors a long time previously who had known God in a real way. He was the same God for them because he is outside of time—that is why in Hebrew he says that he is 'I AM'. That is a very meaningful name or title for God—the one who is always there, without beginning or end, the one who always was and always will be. In fact, the Jewish people saw this as such a revered term for God that they avoided saying the word when they read the Hebrew scriptures and instead said the term 'LORD'. In Hebrew, this name 'I AM' was probably pronounced as 'Yahweh' but in the course of history some people have corrupted it to other pronunciations such as 'Jehovah.'"

"Yes, I agree with you that the important thing is not the name or how you pronounce it but what one understands about the character of God. For me, I find it easier to say 'The God of my fathers' because I think that is more meaningful for me. He is not only the God of the Mongolian peoples but is the God of the whole world, including the Chinese and Turkic peoples."

"That sounds to me like wisdom!"

"Yes, in fact, I'm beginning to think our old saying might be wrong about the wisdom of man being endless. Surely only the wisdom of God is endless!"

"I totally agree."

KARACHAI-CHERKESSIA: RAISING THE DEAD

After arriving in the North Caucasus, I went to visit Osman and Fatima, two Karachai friends of mine. Originally I had met them through attending an academic conference in Nalchik some years previously and I wanted to renew contact with them. They invited me to stay with them in their home in a village in the Republic of Karachai-Cherkessia. One day we travelled together to Dombai and other beautiful parts of the North Caucasus. After a picnic lunch on a mountainside, Osman had walked a little distance away, spread out his prayer rug on the grass and performed his customary *namaz*. It was clear that his faith was very important to him.

The following morning, after a delicious breakfast, we were sitting around the kitchen table when suddenly Osman, my host, started to talk about what he had been reading.

"I've been reading a very interesting passage in the Qur'an," he said, "and there's something I would like to ask you about it."

"What does it say?" I asked.

Osman picked up his Qur'an and began to read from the third *sura*, which is entitled *The Family of Imran*:

> [3.42] And when the angels said: O Marium! surely Allah has chosen you and purified you and chosen you above the women of the world. [3.43] O Marium! keep to obedience to your Lord and humble yourself, and bow down with those who bow.

[3.44] This is of the announcements relating to the unseen which We reveal to you; and you were not with them when they cast their pens (to decide) which of them should have Marium in his charge, and you were not with them when they contended one with another.

[3.45] When the angels said: O Marium, surely Allah gives you good news with a Word from Him (of one) whose name is the Messiah, Isa son of Marium, worthy of regard in this world and the hereafter and of those who are made near (to Allah).

[3.46] And he shall speak to the people when in the cradle and when of old age, and (he shall be) one of the good ones.

[3.47] She said: My Lord! when shall there be a son (born) to me, and man has not touched me? He said: Even so, Allah creates what He pleases; when He has decreed a matter, He only says to it, Be, and it is.

[3.48] And He will teach him the Book and the wisdom and the Tavrat and the Injeel.

[3.49] And (make him) an apostle to the children of Israel: That I have come to you with a sign from your Lord, that I determine for you out of dust like the form of a bird, then I breathe into it and it becomes a bird with Allah's permission and I heal the blind and the leprous, and bring the dead to life with Allah's permission and I inform you of what you should eat and what you should store in your houses; most surely there is a sign in this for you, if you are believers.

[3.50] And a verifier of that which is before me of the *Taurat* and that I may allow you part of that which has been forbidden to you, and I have come to you with a sign from your Lord therefore be careful of (your duty to) Allah and obey me.

[3.51] Surely Allah is my Lord and your Lord, therefore serve Him; this is the right path.

[3.52] But when Isa perceived unbelief on their part, he said Who will be my helpers in Allah's way? The disciples said: We are helpers (in the way) of Allah: We believe in Allah and bear witness that we are submitting ones.

[3.53] Our Lord! we believe in what Thou

hast revealed and we follow the apostle, so write us down with those who bear witness. [3.54] And they planned and Allah (also) planned, and Allah is the best of planners. [3.55] And when Allah said: O Isa, I am going to terminate the period of your stay (on earth) and cause you to ascend unto Me and purify you of those who disbelieve and make those who follow you above those who disbelieve to the day of resurrection; then to Me shall be your return, so I will decide between you concerning that in which you differed.[258]

"That's a very interesting passage, Osman," I remarked. "What is it that you want to ask about it?" I was expecting him to comment on the verses which referred to the miraculous birth of Isa, whereby he was conceived without a human father. Osman's question therefore took me a little by surprise.

"It says here in the Qur'an that Isa Mesih could 'heal the blind and the leprous, and bring the dead to life'. He did that while he was living on this earth but what I want to know is, does he do the same things today?"

"Yes, he does, although I have to admit that it does not seem to happen very often. Even while Isa Mesih was living in this world there were only three dead people that he raised to life, as far as we know. It seems that God sometimes does this miracle as a sign of his power or to confirm that the good news about Isa Mesih is true. God is the one who heals, but often he answers prayers for healing when we pray in the name and authority of Isa Mesih. That is because, as Isa Mesih himself stated, 'All authority in heaven and on earth has been given to me'.[259] That is why Isa Mesih could also give his followers 'authority to drive out evil spirits and to heal every disease and sickness'.[260] Isa Mesih commanded his followers to 'heal the sick, raise the dead, cleanse those who have leprosy' and to 'drive out demons'.[261] Yes, Isa does have authority to heal today too."

"I have heard that Isa Mesih can heal today," replied Osman, "but what about raising the dead? Nowadays, are there any cases in which dead people have been restored to life by Isa Mesih?"

"Yes, there are a number of such cases which I have heard about," I replied. "Would you like me to tell you about some of them?"

"Yes, please, I'm all ears!" responded Osman. Fatima was also listening attentively, so I began to tell them about some cases of the dead being raised to life in modern times.

"Although I have not myself met anyone who has actually been raised to life, in Siberia I have met a follower of Isa Mesih who told me about two people he prayed for who had been raised to life again."

"What happened?" asked Osman.

"Both events happened in the Altai Republic of southern Siberia. In the one case there was someone who had fallen and had been lying on the ground in sub-zero temperatures for about half an hour. People thought he had frozen to death. The other person was someone who had been working on high-voltage electricity cables and had received a powerful electric shock. He fell to the ground and everyone thought he was dead. However, in both cases the man I met in Siberia started to pray to God in the name of Isa Mesih and these people revived."

"Does he have some special power of some kind, then?"

"No, he himself doesn't have the power—although he may have a gift of faith and be able to discern what God wants to do in a certain situation."

"What other examples do you know about then?"

"Another example", I said, "is a case of raising the dead which has been reported from Chile in South America. There a man of God named Andres Montupil visited a house where a girl in her early teens was very ill. As he approached, he could hear the bitter grief of the girl's mother, weeping over the death of her daughter. Andres prayed to God about the situation and then went into the house. Gently he led the girl's mother outside, where there was a clear view of the beautiful Andes mountain range. Andres said to her, 'My Father made this. He is your Father too and he has power to raise up your daughter who is dead—and we're going to pray.' When they went back to the house, the body of the dead child was already cold and stiffening. Andres prayed to God and the others joined in too. At first, nothing was happening so they prayed a second time. Then, when they prayed the third time, Andres said, 'Lord, for your glory, so that these people may know that you exist and that you have power, raise their daughter.' Suddenly the girl coughed and moved. Andres asked the family to give her something to eat and they got her some thin soup. When neighbours who had heard about the death of the child came to console the family, they were astonished to find the child alive."[262]

"That's wonderful," commented Osman, and then asked, "Is that how Isa Mesih raised people when he was in this world too?"

"Definitely!" I replied, "In fact, this example is very reminiscent of the way in which Isa Mesih raised to life a twelve-year old girl. The *Injil* tells us that a man named Jairus

177

came and fell at Isa's feet, pleading with him to come to his house because his only daughter, a girl of about twelve, was dying. However, while Isa Mesih was on the way to see the girl, someone came from the house of Jairus with bad news for him. I picked up the Holy Scriptures and read from the *Injil*:

> "Your daughter is dead," he said. "Don't bother the teacher any more."
>
> Hearing this, Isa said to Jairus, "Don't be afraid; just believe, and she will be healed."
>
> When he arrived at the house of Jairus, he did not let anyone go in with him except Peter, John and James, and the child's father and mother. Meanwhile, all the people were wailing and mourning for her. "Stop wailing," Isa said. "She is not dead but asleep."
>
> They laughed at him, knowing that she was dead. But he took her by the hand and said, "My child, get up!" Her spirit returned, and at once she stood up. Then Isa told them to give her something to eat."[263]

Osman wanted to know more about miracles today. "You told us of one modern example," he said, "but are there any more cases?"

"There are," I replied. "Another modern example of raising the dead to life again comes from South Korea, where a boy named Samuel ate deep-fried silkworms sold by a street vendor. He did not know that the country farmer who had brought the silkworms into the town had used packaging that had previously been used for insecticide. The boy died from the poison.

Samuel's father, Paul Yonggi Cho, is a well-known man of God in Korea. On hearing the news, he returned home and prayed next to the corpse for God to raise his son to life again.

For several hours he remained in prayer until God gave him the gift of faith that Samuel's life would be restored. Then the father loudly shouted the boy's name, 'Samuel!' Clapping his hands together, he cried out, 'Samuel! In the name of Isa Mesih of Nazareth, rise up and walk!'

The boy sprang to his feet, then crumpled and fell half across the bed, vomiting. He gestured with his hand and said, 'Say hello to Isa, Papa.' Again he said, 'Say hello to Isa. He's right there.' The boy pointed. His father bowed toward the place his son was pointing to and said softly, 'Hello, Isa.'

Samuel then said to his father, 'Didn't you see us coming down the hallway? Isa carried me in his arms. He was carrying me to a *beautiful* place—brighter than anything I've ever seen—the most beautiful music my ears have ever heard. I couldn't recognise the tune, but we kept getting closer and closer to it. Then Isa said to me, "We have to go back." "No", I said. "Yes, we have to go back," said Isa, "Your father won't let you go." And he was bringing me back to the bedroom. Didn't you see us coming down the hall? You were calling me and you commanded me to get up. That's when Isa let go of me. There he is—Oh, he's not there—he must have gone back, I guess.'"[264]

"That is a wonderful story," replied Osman, "My Qur'an says that Isa Mesih raises the dead to life. I have never heard of any other prophet who could raise the dead."

"Only God can raise the dead, but he does so in answer to our prayers. He answers the prayers of ordinary people as well as those of prophets. Nevertheless, another prophet who lived about 850 years before Isa Mesih, the prophet Elijah, was also used by God to raise the dead. In fact, the way in which God raised Samuel to life in Korea is very similar to the situation which confronted the prophet Elijah. The prophet Elijah was living with a family when

> the son of the woman who owned the house became ill. He grew worse and worse, and finally stopped breathing. She said to Elijah, 'What do you have against me, man of God? Did you come to remind me of my sin and kill my son?'
>
> 'Give me your son,' Elijah replied. He took him from her arms, carried him to the upper room where he was staying, and laid him on his bed. Then he cried out to the LORD, 'O LORD my God, have you brought tragedy also upon this widow I am staying with, by causing her son to die?' Then he stretched himself out on the boy three times and cried to the LORD, 'O LORD my God, let this boy's life return to him!'
>
> The LORD heard Elijah's cry, and the boy's life returned to him, and he lived. Elijah picked up the child and carried him down from the room into the house. He gave him to his mother and said, 'Look, your son is alive!'
>
> Then the woman said to Elijah, 'Now I know that you are a man of God and that the word of the LORD from your mouth is the truth.'"[265]

"Elijah must have been a great prophet of God," commented Osman, "but all these accounts involve young people who had died not long before being raised to life again in answer to prayer. A sceptic could say that these children were not really dead but only seemed to be dead. What would be far more convincing is an account of someone who had been dead for some days and whose body was already decomposing!"

"You are right, Osman," I replied, "but there are also a few cases of this kind. One such account comes to us from the Democratic Republic of Congo in central Africa, where a man named Alexander was conducting a meeting when the corpse of a young woman was carried in. Her fiancé challenged him with the words, 'You say God raises people from the dead. Here is a test for you.' The woman had already been dead for four days and the stench in the small, stuffy room was almost unbearable. Alexander invited the other believers to gather round and together they lifted their hands in prayer and praise to God. Suddenly, after about twenty minutes, Alexander felt someone tugging at his jacket. He opened his eyes and saw that the corpse was missing. Looking around, he saw the woman who had been dead was standing among those who were praying, with her eyes closed and hands up, praising God!"[266]

"Did Isa Mesih also raise anyone from the dead whose body had already been decomposing?" queried Osman.

"Yes, he did. A similar kind of miracle, involving someone who had been dead a few days, is recorded in the *Injil* concerning Isa Mesih." I read out the passage to him:

> Now a certain man named Lazarus was sick. He was from Bethany, the village where Mary and her sister Martha lived. (Now it was Mary who anointed the Lord with perfumed oil and wiped his feet dry with her hair, whose brother Lazarus was sick.) So the sisters sent a message to Isa, 'Lord, look, the one you love is sick.'

> ...When Isa arrived, he found that Lazarus had been in the tomb four days already. (Now Bethany was less than two miles from Jerusalem, so many of the Jewish people of the region had come to Martha and Mary to console them over the loss of their brother.) So when Martha heard that Isa was coming, she went out to meet him, but Mary was sitting in the house.

Martha said to Isa, 'Lord, if you had been here, my brother would not have died. But even now I know that whatever you ask from God, God will grant you.'

Isa replied, 'Your brother will come back to life again.'

Martha said, 'I know that he will come back to life again in the resurrection at the last day.'

Isa said to her, 'I am the resurrection and the life. The one who believes in me will live even if he dies, and the one who lives and believes in me will never die. Do you believe this?'

She replied, 'Yes, Lord, I believe that you are the Mesih, the Son of God who comes into the world.'

And when she had said this, Martha went and called her sister Mary, saying privately, 'The Teacher is here and is asking for you.' So when Mary heard this, she got up quickly and went to him. (Now Isa had not yet entered the village, but was still in the place where Martha had come out to meet him.) Then the people who were with Mary in the house consoling her saw her get up quickly and go out. They followed her, because they thought she was going to the tomb to weep there.

Now when Mary came to the place where Isa was and saw him, she fell at his feet and said to him, 'Lord, if you had been here, my brother would not have died.'

When Isa saw her weeping, and the people who had come with her weeping, he was intensely moved in spirit and greatly distressed. He asked, 'Where have you laid him?'

They replied, 'Lord, come and see.'

Isa wept. Thus the people who had come to mourn said, 'Look how much he loved him!' But some of them said, 'This is the man who caused the blind man to see! Couldn't he have done something to keep Lazarus from dying?'

Isa, intensely moved again, came to the tomb. (Now it was a cave, and a stone was placed across it.) Isa said, 'Take away the stone.'

Martha, the sister of the deceased, replied, 'Lord, by this time the body will have a bad smell, because he has been buried four days.'

Isa responded, 'Didn't I tell you that if you believe, you would see the glory of God?'

So they took away the stone. Isa looked upward and said, 'Father, I thank you that you have listened to me. I knew that you always listen to me, but I said this for the sake of the crowd standing around here, that they may believe that you sent me.'

When he had said this, he shouted in a loud voice, 'Lazarus, come out!' The one who had died came out, his feet and hands tied up with strips of cloth, and a cloth wrapped around his face.

Isa said to them, 'Unwrap him and let him go.'"[267]

"Wow!" gasped Osman. "It must be practically impossible to explain away accounts of raising to life again someone who has been dead three or four days." He paused, then continued, "Nevertheless, I suppose sceptics may still say that perhaps the person was not 'really' dead and had simply revived in the tomb. Are there any cases in which a doctor has verified that the person was actually dead?"

"In many parts of the world the local people are very familiar with death and can recognise the symptoms of death even if a doctor has not confirmed that the person is dead," I replied. "However, in some cases a doctor has indeed confirmed that all clinical signs of life were absent, and from a medical perspective the person was dead. Such was the case for a child named Katshinyi, who had died in a hospital in Africa and for whom the doctors had even written out the death certificate. Later that same day a man of God named Mahash Chavda was addressing a crowd in the central square of the city when God told him that that there was someone there whose son had died that morning. Just at that time Katshinyi's father, whose name was Mulamba, came to the square and heard what the man of God was saying. The man of God prayed with Mulamba, asking God to raise the dead boy back to life. At that very moment, in the hospital morgue, the dead body suddenly moved; the boy sneezed, sat up and asked for food."[268]

"Well, if a person is really dead, of course it is impossible to explain away the healing in conventional medical terms. We cannot say that the dead person got better because of medicines or anything like that!" remarked Osman.

"You are right. The only possible way to explain it away in human terms is to assert that the person was not really dead but only seemed to be. However, such an attitude is like that of an ostrich who refuses to look at the facts. From any normal perspective, the people described in these accounts were either dead or else were so seriously ill that they would not have been able to recover in such a way as to convince those around that God had raised them from the dead."

Fatima had been listening intently and now she raised a question.

"But why does God raise some people to life and not others?" she asked. "Why are there only a small number of such cases?"

"That is a good question but it is not an easy one to answer, because God alone knows why he chooses to restore some people to life in this world while others go to their eternal destiny. What we can say, however, is that all these people who had been raised to life in answer to prayer were given some more time to live on this earth. However, eventually they too have died or will die, even if it is from a different type of illness or simply from old age. We have to assume that God has a specific purpose for them to continue to live in this life."

"Do these people who were raised from the dead say what they have seen in the other world?" asked Osman.

"Sometimes they do—like Samuel in Korea who said that he was being carried by Isa Mesih to a beautiful and bright place with most beautiful music. Other accounts do not mention the details. However, even if we can learn from these accounts about what they have seen during their brief glimpse of the life to come, what is a far more important issue is that we too need to be ready to meet with God after our own deaths. What will we say to our Creator?"

"You are right!" exclaimed Osman. "And that is why this passage from the Qur'an is so important. Here it is written that Isa Mesih went back to God in heaven. He came from God and he went back to heaven, so he must know the way there!"

"You are a man of great insight, Osman," I agreed. "In fact, Isa Mesih spoke about the place which he was preparing in heaven for those who love and follow him. He said, 'Do not let your hearts be troubled. Trust in God; trust also in me. In my Father's house are many rooms; if it were not so, I would have told you. I am going there to prepare a place for you. And if I go and prepare a place for you, I will come back and take you to be with me that you also may be where I am.'"[269]

"Like He did with that young boy in Korea!" remarked Osman.

"Yes, but Isa Mesih also said to his followers, 'You know the way to the place where I am going.'"[270]

"They might have known the way, but we don't!" commented Osman.

"Actually, that was more or less the reaction of one of Isa Mesih's followers too. He said to Isa Mesih, 'Lord, we don't know where you are going, so how can we know the way?'[271] How do you think Isa Mesih answered him?"

"I don't know," replied Osman.

I picked up the *Injil* and quoted the passage giving Isa Mesih's answers. "He said, 'I am the way and the truth and the life. No-one comes to the Father except through me.'"[272]

Osman was thoughtful for a moment, then said, "No-one comes to God except through Isa Mesih? No other prophet made that kind of a claim—not even our own prophet, who, in the sura entitled 'The Sandhills', said, 'I am not the first of the apostles, and I do not know what will be done with me or with you: I do not follow anything but that which is revealed to me, and I am nothing but a plain warner.'"[273]

Fatima spoke up, saying: "But also no other prophet was raised to life again like Isa Mesih! So of course he knows the way to heaven!"

"Was the resurrection of Isa Mesih like these accounts of raising the dead that you have told us about?" asked Osman.

"No, these accounts of raising the dead are quite different from what happened to Isa Mesih after he died and returned to life again. His resurrection body was of a totally different kind. It was a new body with new and different properties. It was no longer bounded by walls—but the new body of Isa Mesih was not like a ghost because he could eat and drink with his friends, and even cook breakfast for them. It was a tangible body which could be clung on to. He invited one of his friends, who doubted that Isa Mesih had been raised from death, to put his hands in the nail wounds in order to verify that it really was Isa Mesih. The difference was that this new body would never die again. After forty days, Isa Mesih was taken up to heaven but one day he will return to this world to judge it. However, first he came to save the world by giving each of us an opportunity to put our trust in him as the One who can deliver us from hell and give us eternal life in heaven."

Osman looked at Fatima, then commented, "I had never really previously understood this passage from the Qur'an, but now it makes so much more sense. I now realise how important it is to know more about Isa Mesih, because in the Qur'an Allah says to Isa Mesih that Allah would 'make those who follow you above those who disbelieve to the day of resurrection'. I for one *do* want to believe in Isa Mesih on the day of resurrection."

KISLOVODSK: SPORT IN THE CAUCASUS

Early one morning, I went for a run in the forested hills next to the resort town of Kislovodsk. Getting out into the hills when few others were around was a wonderful opportunity to enjoy the beauty of God's creation. Some of it was still shrouded by the early morning mist but at this time in the morning there are other treasures to be seen which are likely to disappear when the sun gains its strength. For example, the beautiful spider's web, stretched across the path, is a work of art. The design itself is so intricate that it points to the Creator's hand in fashioning the spider with such skill. In this case, the Creator himself then added the early morning dew drops to make it glisten in the sunlight. An hour or so later, the beauty is likely to have disappeared and the web itself destroyed by someone walking into it.

All around us the Creator is designing new works of art which few besides the Creator himself are even aware of. God delights in variety: his works carry the stamp of an artist. Just as an artist may produce many similar pictures but each one is different in some way from the others, so God makes each of his creations unique. We can see that uniqueness in each of us—in our fingerprints, the patterns of the iris in our eyes, even the shape of our ears. Each tiger has a unique pattern of stripes on the face. Most snowflakes are different. Stars are different. The whole of God's creation points to an artistic touch which delights in uniqueness.

As I came running back down the hill towards the 'sanatorium' where I was staying, I noticed a man watching me. I had met Ramza the previous day and had spent the evening together with him. He was a Chechen man who during the war had lost his home in Grozny and now lived in another city, outside of Chechnya itself. I enjoyed talking with him but our conversation had come to a sudden halt as soon as the wrestling started on the television.

"Good for you!" remarked Ramza, surprised to see me running.

"I suppose round here not many grandfathers go jogging, do they?" I replied. (I had already told him that I have two granddaughters.)

"No—we prefer other types of sport, and the old men just watch."

"Yes, the people of the Caucasus love to watch wrestling, don't they?"

"And to take part in it, at least when we are younger."

"I expect there was great rejoicing during the Olympics when once again wrestlers from Dagestan got gold medals—not only in Athens but then in Beijing."

"You mean Mavlet Batirov and Buvaysak Saytiev? Did you know that they were both born in Khasavyurt in Dagestan?"

"I did know that. And there was another wrestler who was born in Nalchik. What was his name?"

"You must mean Aslanbek Khushtov. He also got a gold in Beijing."

"I heard that Dagestani wrestlers got three golds and one silver medal in Beijing. I don't know the nationalities of all the wrestlers but it seemed to me that people from the Caucasus dominated the wrestling once again."

"Yes—even the gold medallist representing Uzbekistan, Artur Taymazov, was actually born in Vladikavkaz!"

"Kazakstan, Kyrgyzstan and Azerbaijan also got some silver and bronze medals, didn't they?"

"Yes, and Tajikistan too—but do you know where their silver medallist in wrestling, Yusup Abdusalomov, was born?"

"No. But it sounds like he might be from the Caucasus too!"

"Makhachkala!"

"So, another Dagestani! But wrestling is popular all over the Caucasus, not only in Dagestan, isn't it?"

"Sure, even the Georgians are good at it. They got some medals too—even a couple of golds."

"In the Olympics people were focussing so much on the nationality of each competitor but all of them did fantastically. They all deserved their medals. What is really important is not their nationality so much as their character and discipline."

"They need discipline but what do you mean about their character?"

"That's all wrapped up with the discipline. Day after day they have spent long hours in training and practising their skills. Their success does not come without discipline. There is a cost to every reward. In this case, the cost can be counted in terms of what they have given up for the sake of discipline and commitment to their cause. Maybe they would like to have spent their time doing something less strenuous—maybe watching TV, visiting friends or even just staying longer in bed! However, they have chosen to give up or reduce some activities, which may be good in themselves, so that they can focus on what for them is more important."

"I'd never before thought about what they might have had to give up."

"There is a cost to everything in life. In fact, God himself wants us to live our lives with the same kind of discipline as we see in the lives of our sportsmen and women."

"Really? I thought God didn't like sports!"

"Why do you think that?"

"Well, the Qur'an doesn't say much about sports but what it does say seems rather disparaging."

"What does it say?"

"For example, one place says that 'this world's life is naught but a play and an idle sport'.[274] Elsewhere the Qur'an mentions those who 'take their religion for an idle sport and a play and this life's world deceives them'.[275] Another verse says: 'this life of the world is nothing but a sport and a play; and as for the next abode, that most surely is the life'."[276]

"But the Qur'an does not say that sport is a sin! Rather, its emphasis is on the importance of the spiritual life. In this, there is agreement between the Qur'an and the *Injil*, where it is written that 'physical training is of some value, but godliness has value for all things, holding promise for both the present life and the life to come.'"[277]

"So why did you say that God himself wants us to live our lives like sportsmen and women?"

"What I said was that he wants us to have the same kind of discipline as we see in their lives—and also in the lives of people who take part in many other kinds of sports, including the Paralympics. In saying this, I had in mind some of the positive features of sport which are also praised in the *Injil*. For example, the *Injil* tells us that God trains us in the same way as sportsmen are trained. It gives the example of running in a race. Just as a runner needs to wear light clothing so as to run faster, we too need to put aside the wrong things in our lives which hinder our spiritual progress. It is written: 'Let us throw off everything that hinders and the sin that so easily entangles, and let us run with perseverance the race marked out for us.'"[278]

"Do you mean that life is like a race?"

"Yes, or like any other kind of sport, really. However, this passage in the *Injil* then continues by pointing us to a greater example of fortitude and patience in the face of hardship—namely, Isa Mesih. The next words after those just quoted go on to say: 'Let us fix our eyes on Isa, the author and perfecter of our faith, who for the joy set before him endured the cross, scorning its shame, and sat down at the right hand of the throne of God. Consider him who endured such opposition from sinful men, so that you will not grow weary and lose heart.'"[279]

"I once saw a film about Isa Mesih and I was amazed at how much Isa Mesih suffered from the flogging and the crucifixion. You could probably say that he endured far more suffering than any of our boxers or wrestlers: at least, their fights are bounded by rules and do not normally lead to death!"

"That's true. So the example of Isa Mesih can inspire us to carry on living as God wants us to, in spite of misunderstanding or opposition by those who do not want our pure lives to show up the dirt and darkness in their lives. It is written in the *Injil*:

> This is the verdict: Light has come into the world, but men loved darkness instead of light because their deeds were evil. Everyone who does evil hates the light, and will not come into the light for fear that his deeds will be exposed. But whoever lives by the truth comes into the light, so that it may be seen plainly that what he has done has been done through God.[280]"

"What has that to do with sport? I don't see what you mean."

"In a race, we can be inspired to go on to the finishing line by seeing the example of those who have endured to the end and completed it. In the same way, in this corrupt world where there are so many temptations to do wrong, it is not easy to live a pure and honest life. If you want to live by God's standards of integrity and purity, you are likely to be misunderstood. If you refuse to give in to the corrupt standards of other people, they may oppose you because your honest and righteous life shows up the deceitfulness and dishonesty in their lives. Our sportsmen who want to win a gold medal in the Olympics not only have to undergo discipline and training but they also need to overcome the opposition. We too have a spiritual opponent—Satan and his demonic servants. In that spiritual fight against the powers of darkness, we too need to have discipline and the right training."

"So where does it end? Do we get a medal for struggling against Satan?"

"In one sense, yes. In the Olympic games nowadays, the victors receive medals but in the original Olympic games, when they first started in ancient Greece, the victors were given a wreath of olive branches.[281] The Romans used laurel wreaths to symbolise victory. From this was derived the practice of kings wearing crowns on their heads.[282] The *Injil* refers to such wreaths or crowns in several places, saying that God will give rewards to those who are faithful in following Isa Mesih. It is written, for example: 'Blessed is the man who perseveres under trial, because when he has stood the test, he will receive the crown of life that God has promised to those who love him.'[283] That is why a faithful follower of Isa Mesih could write, towards the end of his life: '... I have finished the race, I have kept the faith. Now there is in store for me the crown of righteousness, which the Lord, the righteous Judge, will award to me on that day—and not only to me, but also to all who have longed for his appearing.'[284]"

"So do you mean that only those who have done the best get the spiritual equivalent of gold or silver medals? I suppose most of us don't have a chance."

"Actually, this crown or laurel wreath—that is, the equivalent of an Olympic 'gold medal'—is given to those who have been faithful in spite of difficulty or hardship. Like sportsmen today, we have to be prepared to endure hardship in order to win the prize. Unlike the Olympics, there is a prize for all who complete the course, not just for the one who gets there first. God rewards those who do not give up. Isa Mesih made a promise to some people living in what is now Turkey, saying, 'Be faithful, even to the point of death, and I will give you the crown of life.'"[285]

"To the point of death? That's hard!"

"But death is only the doorway to a life in eternity! In the light of eternity, each of us has to make a decision about the way we live our lives now. Are we willing to run the race of life in the way that God wants us to? Are we willing to endure hardship so that we can obtain that eternal prize which God gives those who endure to the end?"

"Yes, endurance is one thing, but is that all it takes to reach heaven?"

"No—just like a sportsman only receives the prize by obeying the rules. Athletes can be disqualified if they take certain kinds of steroids or drugs to enhance performance. Even if they have won a race, they lose the prize if they have cheated. In the same way, we too need to observe the rules of life which God has created for the good of all. These rules are explained in God's holy books."

"But it is so hard to live according to all the rules in God's books! Do this, don't do that! It's virtually impossible!"

"That's why we need a spiritual trainer! Our sportsmen didn't get their medals just by observing the rules in the book! They need a physical trainer who comes alongside the athlete to help the athlete to do even better. The trainer encourages the sportsman in good habits but also corrects the athlete's mistakes. In the same way, God sends his Holy Spirit to help us to live in the way that God wants—to be like the athlete who runs according the rules and is not disqualified for the prize."

"I had never heard before of God actually helping us to live our lives better."

"Several centuries before the time of Isa Mesih, the prophet Jeremiah spoke the following words from God:

'This is the covenant I will make with the house of Israel after that time,' declares the LORD. 'I will put my law in their minds and write it on their hearts. I will be their God, and they will be my people.

No longer will a man teach his neighbour, or a man his brother, saying, "Know the LORD," because they will all know me, from the least of them to the greatest,' declares the LORD. 'For I will forgive their wickedness and will remember their sins no more'."[286]

"Do you really mean that?" interjected Ramza. "That is an amazing promise! Are you saying that God promises that he will forgive people's sins and even forget about them!"

"That is what is says! You can pray right now and ask God to make you clean, to forgive your wrongdoings and even to remember your sins no more. However, there is even more. God promises to put his law in our minds and write it on our hearts. How does he do this? Isa Mesih explained how this happens. Isa Mesih promised to send his Holy Spirit to live with us and to teach us the ways of God. He said, 'the Counsellor, the Holy Spirit, whom the Father will send in my name, will teach you all things and will remind you of everything I have said to you'.[287]

Isa Mesih promised to send us the Holy Spirit as a trainer for our spiritual lives. The question each of us has to think about is whether or not we are willing to invite God's Holy Spirit to become our spiritual trainer or mentor. If that is what we want to do, we can talk to God now in our own words and invite him to help us in this."

"I don't really know what to say to him. I only know the words of the prayers I have been taught. Can you give me an example of what to do or say?"

"If you want, you could say the following kind of prayer:

'Holy God, you call us to live a disciplined, godly life but I am not like a disciplined Olympic sportsman. I have failed you and not lived my life according to your rules. Please forgive me. Please send your Holy Spirit to live in me and to teach me your ways of holiness, truth and love. I want to live by your standards and by your truth even if it hurts and even if others misunderstand me. Please take my life and transform it, so that I may live your way and not my own way.'"

DAGESTAN: ANGELS

From Nalchik in the Kabardino-Balkar Republic, I was able to join a tour bus going southwards into the heart of the Caucasus mountains. The route was a beautiful one, gradually ascending to higher elevations. Finally, we stopped at a car park where one could take a chair lift up the mountain. I paid the fee and went up to the first stage, where there was already a good view of the surrounding mountainous scenery. A woman came up to me to offer hand-knitted woollen jumpers for sale. They were certainly nice and warm—just what one needs for these kinds of altitudes. I told her that I would think about it and perhaps have a look at them again on my way down.

There was a second chair lift up to an even higher altitude. The bus driver had warned the passengers to be careful of altitude sickness and not to go to the second level if they were not used to such altitudes. I felt that I was not going to miss out on the opportunity to see this wonderful scenery! In any case, I was used to living at a relatively high altitude so I decided to go on up.

From the summit there was a view across to Mount Elbruz—the highest peak in the Caucasus. It was the principal jewel set in a crown of magnificent mountain peaks.

I was glad to have had the opportunity to glimpse this majestic peak, even though clouds swirled around it, often obscuring it for a while. Often our experience of the spiritual realm is like that. We catch a glimpse of spiritual realities but then it is again covered by the 'clouds' of daily life. Nevertheless, those moments of insight, of seeing behind the obscuring clouds, remain treasured memories which can change our whole outlook on life.

Such a moment of insight once happened to a friend of mine named Irina. By nationality she is Bashkort—though the Russians refer to her people as Bashkirs—but in terms of religion she regarded herself as an atheist.

One day Irina phoned me and said that she now believes there is a God because she had seen an angel. The angel had been hovering over her while she was ill. Irina felt that the angel was protecting and comforting her. At first she was afraid to tell some of her friends about her experience for fear that they would laugh at her or think she was deluded. That was why she decided to phone me, because she wanted to talk with someone who would understand and would take her seriously.

Through this experience Irina had come to believe that there is a God—but she did not know what else to believe. In her own words, she expressed this by saying that she did not know whether she should become "a Buddhist or a Baptist"! Nevertheless, her experience made her want to read the Holy Books and to think about these questions for herself with an open mind. Eventually she came into a personal relationship with God and experienced a sense of having been forgiven and of having been made clean inside her spirit.

Irina recognised that what she had seen was an angel because it fitted the classical pictures of angels as beings with wings. There are different kinds of angels and it seems that they differ in their appearance. The prophet Isaiah saw angels with six wings and he described his vision as follows:

> I saw the Lord seated on a throne, high and exalted, and the train of his robe filled the temple. Above him were

seraphs, each with six wings: With two wings they covered their faces, with two they covered their feet, and with two they were flying. And they were calling to one another:

"Holy, holy, holy is the LORD Almighty;
the whole earth is full of his glory."

At the sound of their voices the doorposts and thresholds shook and the temple was filled with smoke.

"Woe to me!" I cried. "I am ruined! For I am a man of unclean lips, and I live among a people of unclean lips, and my eyes have seen the King, the LORD Almighty."[288]

The angels described here were apparently ones who were close to God and who were at that time engaged in worship. It is interesting that with two of their wings 'they covered their faces'. A Kyrgyz woman who thought about this passage commented to me that it is similar to the Central Asian custom of putting one's hands to one's face after praying. She wondered if the custom might even have come from the same origin.

However, not all angels appear to us in this form. An example of an angel whose appearance was without wings, and like that of an ordinary man, was related to me when I travelled on to Dagestan. There I met a Lak man named Nurettin, who told me about a stranger who unexpectedly helped him in his time of need and then mysteriously disappeared. His story is as follows.

"One night my son Saidin had a serious fall and broke his back," related Nurettin. "He tried to stand up but couldn't do so... His legs were paralysed. It was when he was six or seven years old.

"He lay in hospital and my wife was with him... I was out of work apart from doing some odd jobs, and my wife was a hairdresser so we didn't have much income. We had to sell our apartment to pay for the hospital fees. A friend said he would pray for Saidin at the place where they had their meeting. I went there one Thursday evening. About forty to fifty people were there and my friend introduced me to the pastor. When I told him about my problem, he said, 'Do you believe that Isa Mesih is the Creator of all?' I thought he was rude and asked why he asked this. Then I went to the Muslims and asked them to help Saidin—but that didn't seem to help either.

"After going to the mosque, I went back to the church. The pastor said he would pray in the name of Isa Mesih. I didn't know what would happen but I didn't understand. I didn't want him to put his hands on me while they prayed but I endured it patiently because he was giving help. While they were praying, a woman had a revelation that there was a curse on *me*—not on my son. If there is a revelation from God, you should pray about it. They said they would pray for both myself and my son. The pastor also said to me, 'You yourself have got to ask God too' I replied, 'I don't know your prayers; all I know are the Arabic ritual prayers.' He replied, 'He is God and doesn't need special words, but he needs sincerity and honesty in your heart.' Later on, at home, when I was alone for the first time, I prayed to the Most High. I didn't know how to pray. I just went on my knees and began to pray what was on my heart—a cry of despair: 'Allah, in the name of Isa Mesih I don't want my son to be an invalid. If you hear, in the name of Isa Mesih I ask for my son to be saved.'

"At the hospital, the staff would accept presents of chocolates, champagne or money if they thought there was at least some hope of the patient's recovery—but they were not accepting our presents. This showed that they thought there was no hope for him. There was nothing they could do for Saidin. By that time I was emotionally drained, and felt that my strength had been sapped too."

"Then the surgeon said that they could try to operate and clean out the haematoma. However, we would have to wait a long time. The only way to get the operation done quicker would be to get the signatures of the Minister of Health and of other high officials so as to get priority treatment. I was given a piece of paper with details of the necessary operation and was looking at it in the hospital when suddenly I was approached by an old man wearing old-fashioned dress, like that at the time of the First World War. Suddenly he snatched the paper out of my hand and went away with it before I could react. I didn't know what to do. I had no idea where this person had gone so I thought perhaps it was better to wait where I was in the corridor next to the stairs. A little while later this same person came up to me and put the paper back in my hand. He went off down the corridor. I looked at the paper and on it were the signatures of the Minister of Health and of other senior doctors! I turned to my friend and said, 'That's the man who took my paper.' However, when I looked back down the corridor, there was nobody there! There were three doors at the end of that corridor but when we tried them, we found that all of them were locked!

"Later, when I showed the paper to people at the hospital, they commented that I must have very high connections or be a relative of someone in the government—but I am not! No relatives had helped me, but I then went back to the meeting of the followers of Isa Mesih and thanked them for their prayers. They again prayed for me and my son.

"On the day before the doctors wanted to operate on Saidin, the doors of his ward were shut but he saw a person come to him. A strong light was coming from that person's clothes. Saidin couldn't see the man's face: it was so bright. When he looked at the man, Saidin felt no pain. The visitor said to him, 'Don't allow yourself to worry. I myself will heal you'. Then the visitor went out. The next day they were going to operate but he said, 'Don't disturb me: I'm healed!' Suddenly his legs moved and came up. The doctor postponed the operation because he couldn't do it to someone in such a condition.

"Prior to the day set for the postponed operation, the swellings on my son's spine had disappeared. Later the hospital again took X-rays of my son's spine—and they could not find any fracture! They took eight pictures on the same day—which is usually forbidden, as normally there should be six months between photos. My wife was angry with them and asked why they had taken so many X-rays. They replied that they had wanted to find the fracture, but they couldn't find it: there was no break!

"I told the people at the fellowship about it. Many rejoiced. My son asked me to buy him some trainers and sports gear. It was expensive for me but I agreed to do so and bought them myself. Saidin was very glad. About a month and a half later I went to the hospital to bring food for my wife and my son, and asked one of the staff to call my wife to the visiting area. Eventually she came but she had someone with her. At first I thought she was looking after someone else's child too: I didn't recognise my own son! My wife was smiling and with a quiet voice said, 'You see: he is walking!'

"After that, my son began to walk better and better and to lift his legs. At first his muscles were weak but now he can run and jump. The doctors said that both his legs are now normal."

After Nurettin had finished his story I asked him about the man who took his paper and got all the signatures on it. "Do you think he was an angel?" I asked Nurettin.

204

"Yes, I think so," he replied.

In this case, the angel did not fit the stereotype of a being in white with wings. However, it is clear from the Holy Books that sometimes God sends angels who look just like ordinary human beings. For example, in the *Taurat* there is an account of the prophet Ibrahim welcoming visitors who looked like human beings but then turned out to be angels. Two of these visitors then went to rescue the prophet Ibrahim's nephew Lut and his family from the city of Sodom before it was destroyed.[289] To Lut and the people of Sodom, these visitors looked like ordinary men but in fact they were angels with supernatural power and authority given by God so they could help Lut.[290]

The *Injil* declares: "Are not all angels ministering spirits sent to serve those who will inherit salvation?"[291] Angels are servants of God who minister in many different ways but usually they are unseen by ordinary human beings. At times, however, God may open our eyes to see the presence of glorious angels around us. At other times God may send angels who look like human beings in order to help us in particular ways.

However, angels, like human beings, can make choices. They are not robots. God's great love is such that he allows both human beings and angels to choose whether or not to worship and serve him. Some angels chose to rebel against God and they were thrown out of heaven. Their leader is Satan—and his angelic helpers are known in different languages as demons, jinn, evil spirits or dirty spirits. It is written in the *Injil*:

> And there was war in heaven. Michael and his angels fought against the dragon, and the dragon and his angels fought back. But he was not strong enough and they

lost their place in heaven. The great dragon was hurled down—that ancient serpent called the devil or Satan, who leads the whole earth astray. He was hurled to the earth, and his angels with him.[292]

In the unseen, spiritual realm there is also a conflict going on between the powers of good and evil. This same struggle is reflected also in our visible world. We too have a choice to make. Are we willing to submit ourselves to God's authority, or will we rebel against God's ways? In other words, will we choose to join in Satan's rebellion against God or will we align ourselves with God and his holy angels? The choice is ours.

Demons or 'dirty spirits' can affect us in many ways, including causing mental or physical sickness. Satan wants us to serve him in hell rather than enjoying fellowship with God in heaven. That is why Satan wants us to die without knowing a real relationship with God and the forgiveness of sins.

However, God did not leave us defenceless against the devil. Who in this world has authority to cast dirty spirits out of people or to heal sicknesses caused by demons? Who is the one who can raise dead people back to life? Only Isa Mesih has this authority, but he shares it with those who belong to him. In the name of Isa Mesih, demons can be cast out from people. Isa Mesih comes to bring the Kingdom of heaven to us here.

Isa Mesih came to destroy the works of the evil one.[293] Think back to the story which Nurettin told about the healing of his son. Who do you think was the being who visited Nurettin's son and whose clothes were shining brightly with a strong light? Was that an angel too? A clue is given by the words spoken by this visitor to Saidin, saying, "I myself will heal you". God can send angels to bring comfort and peace to people but the one who heals is God, not angels. God says, "I am the Lord who heals you".[294] Therefore this visitor to Saidin must be One who is greater than an angel. Saidin's description of his visitor reminds us of the following passage in the *Injil*:

> ...Isa took with him Peter, James and John the brother of James, and led them up a high mountain by themselves. There he was transfigured before them. His face shone like the sun, and his clothes became as white as the light. Just then there appeared before them Musa and Elijah, talking with Isa.[295]

Usually Isa Mesih also looked like an ordinary man but on this occasion his followers were given a glimpse of his true nature. He was talking with two great prophets, Musa and Elijah, who had lived centuries before Isa Mesih. However, their clothes were not dazzling white like those of Isa Mesih.

Isa Mesih was not an angel but in fact he is greater than the angels. It is written: 'After he had provided purification for sins, he sat down at the right hand of the Majesty in heaven. So he became as much superior to the angels as the name he has inherited is superior to theirs.'[296]

Isa Mesih is now in heaven, seated at the right hand of God, but for a while he became a human being and lived among us. During this time he had the authority to call on many thousands of angels to help him, if he wanted to do so.[297] However, he chose not to use that authority! Why? Above all else he was thinking about our good—because for our sakes he chose to allow himself to go into the devil's realm![298] Even hell itself could not hold the pure, sinless Isa Mesih.

The *Injil* explains it as follows:

> Since the children have flesh and blood, he too shared in their humanity so that by his death he might destroy

him who holds the power of death—that is, the devil—
and free those who all their lives were held in slavery by
their fear of death. For surely it is not angels he helps, but
Ibrahim's descendants.[299]

God raised Isa Mesih from the dead and he is 'now
crowned with glory and honour because he suffered death, so
that by the grace of God he might taste death for everyone.'[300]

Isa Mesih came to set us free from the results of demonic
activity in our lives so that we can live in the way that God
intends. If we want to be on God's side and to turn away from
living under the influence of Satan and his demonic forces,
we can pray the following prayer:

"Holy God, you are the Almighty One, the creator of
the universe, including angels. I am sorry that I have allowed
myself to listen to the temptations and deceptions of evil and
dirty spirits. Please set me free from the lies of Satan so that
I may hear your voice. I want to serve you and to be on the
side of your holy angels. I thank you that the Lord Isa Mesih
conquered the powers of darkness when he died and then
overcome death by being raised to life again. Thank you that
by the authority of Isa Mesih I can be set free from slavery to
demons and from the fear of death. Please forgive me for all
the wrong in my life and set me free by your power to live for
you and your glory."

AZERBAIJAN: THE
PROPHET IN WHITE

Travelling southwards from Makhachkala, I passed through Derbent—the gateway to the Caucasus from the south, which since ancient times had guarded the narrow strip of land between the sea and the mountains. I was nearing the end of my pilgrimage and was keen to reach my destination. However, the meaning of pilgrimage is not so much the final destination as the journey itself. People are more important than places. That is why I wanted to take time out from the main route along the coastal plain so as to visit a Tabassaran man whom I had met in Kislovodsk and who had invited me to visit him if ever I had an opportunity to do so. He lived in a village in the mountains but he met me after my arrival in Derbent and drove me in his car up to his village.

The last fifty kilometres or more was along an unpaved, bumpy road. At one point we had to stop and wait for a flock of sheep to move. They were blocking the road but they were obediently following their shepherd.

While we waited for the sheep to pass, my Tabassaran friend turned to me and said, "This always reminds me of the wonderful song in the *Zabur*, composed by the prophet Davud, which tells us that God is like our shepherd."

Before I had a chance to comment, he began to recite the song from memory:

"The LORD is my shepherd, I shall lack nothing.
He makes me lie down in green pastures,

> he leads me beside quiet waters, he restores my soul.
> He guides me in paths of righteousness for his name's
> sake.
> Even though I walk through the valley of the shadow of
> death,
> I will fear no evil, for you are with me;
> your rod and your staff, they comfort me.
> You prepare a table before me in the presence of my
> enemies.
> You anoint my head with oil; my cup overflows.
> Surely goodness and love will follow me all the days of
> my life,
> and I will dwell in the house of the LORD for ever."[301]

I knew that my Tabassaran friend loved the Holy Scriptures but I could not always remember them as accurately as he could. I opened the *Injil* and from it read some words which Isa Mesih had said about himself:

> "I am the good shepherd. The good shepherd lays down his life for the sheep. The hired hand is not the shepherd who owns the sheep. So when he sees the wolf coming, he abandons the sheep and runs away. Then the wolf attacks the flock and scatters it. The man runs away because he is a hired hand and cares nothing for the sheep. I am the good shepherd; I know my sheep and the sheep know me—just as the Father knows me and I know the Father—and I lay down my life for the sheep."[302]

Like going to spend time with my Tabassaran friend, pilgrimage is not just a journey *to* a special holy place. Instead, it is a walk *with* God. However, my friend is not with me all the time, whereas God is always with us. Our walk with God is supposed to be like that of the sheep with their shepherd on their annual journey up to the higher pastures in the mountains. Their journey is a regular part of life, not just a special journey perhaps once in a lifetime. Every day is an opportunity to walk with God. In this sense of the word, every day can be a pilgrimage.

Eventually the time came for me to return to the coastal road on my way towards Azerbaijan. As I said farewell to my friend, he asked me if I had a map. I assured him that I did.

"Yes, I thought you would—just like you have your spiritual map with you too!" he remarked. His love for the Holy Scriptures was obvious and I respected the way in which he used God's holy books as a guidebook or map on the journey of life, so that he would not get spiritually or morally lost. It was clear that, from reading God's Holy Books, he understood what life is all about and how to walk in God's ways.

I felt sad leaving him and his family, knowing that the final part of my journey would be on my own. However, I was not totally alone, as I still had with me the guide about whom I had spoken with Jamshed in Tajikistan.

God nevertheless prepared other companions for me along the way—people whom I met on the bus. I was invited by an Azeri man named Vasif to spend the night at his home. It was in an area in the north of Azerbaijan where many of the local people belong to the Lezghin nationality, but Vasif himself is Azeri.

When we arrived at Vasif's house, his wife was sitting at a loom weaving a traditional carpet. I noticed that the motif was one of three crosses arranged in a line.

Vasif introduced me to his wife as a pilgrim.

"If you are on a pilgrimage, where are you going to?" she asked.

"I am on the same kind of pilgrimage as the prophet Ibrahim," I replied.

"Where was he going?" she queried.

"Originally he lived in a city in what is now Iraq but God called the prophet to move to another land, where Ibrahim had no permanent dwelling but instead lived in tents as a nomad. I'm not living in a tent because you have very kindly offered me hospitality in your home. However, the state of Ibrahim's heart was that of a pilgrim. He was prepared to become a nomad in this world because he knew that God had a much better dwelling place prepared for him in heaven. In the Holy Book it is written:

> By faith Ibrahim, when called to go to a place he would later receive as his inheritance, obeyed and went, even though he did not know where he was going. By faith he made his home in the promised land like a stranger in a foreign country; he lived in tents, as did Isaak and Yakub, who were heirs with him of the same promise. For he was looking forward to the city with foundations, whose architect and builder is God.[303]"

Vasif was curious about this and asked, "Where is this city which God has made?"

"The prophet knew that his pilgrimage does not end in this life," I explained. "The final destination of the pilgrim is heaven—the city of God. That is also the true place of pilgrimage for all of us. God is calling each one of us to be a pilgrim in this world—but the true pilgrimage of the soul is much harder than that of a physical journey to another country. Our pilgrimage demands discipline of our minds and endurance in our spirits. God commands us: 'Set your minds on things above, not on earthly things.'[304] God wants our attitude to the things of this world to be like that of a pilgrim, who is passing through on the way to the holy city. We are not to be engrossed in the temporal things of this world which perish and fade. Instead we should be like pilgrims in this world and should fix our eyes on the eternal realities of the city to which God is calling us. That is the true meaning of pilgrimage."

"A pilgrim of that kind is very welcome in our home," responded Vasif.

"Peace be upon this house," I replied.

Vasif and his wife were very generous in their hospitality. I also noticed how Vasif was very religious and made an effort to pray during the daytime at the customary times, even though he admitted that sometimes he did miss out some of the times of prayer.

"When you pray, has God ever spoken to you?" I asked.

Vasif seemed surprised at the question.

"No—why should he speak to someone like me?" he replied. "I am not a prophet!"

I glanced across at Vasif's little son, playing quietly on the rug.

"You love your son Sadiq to talk with you, don't you?" I replied.

"Of course! I love to chat with him about the things that are important to him. It's lovely when he asks me questions and I can explain things to him."

"Don't you think God thinks the same about our relationship with him?" I asked. "God created mankind to have a relationship with him. At the beginning Adam and Eve had that close friendship with God when they walked and talked together in the garden, but unfortunately it was lost because of their sin. Nevertheless, God wants each one of us to spend time not only talking to him but also listening to him."

"I had never thought of it that way before," admitted Vasif. "But how do we hear from God? Does he speak in some kind of loud voice?"

"God can speak to us in many different ways. Most important of all is through the holy scriptures. If we read all of God's holy books, including the *Taurat*, the *Zabur* and the *Injil*, we can recognise the voice of God speaking to our hearts. I always ask God to speak to me through the holy books whenever I start to read. It is good to make it a daily practice to read a portion of the holy books every day, even if it is just a chapter or a page."

"Of course God has spoken through the prophets, and I agree it is very important to read what has been spoken though them, but I thought you were talking about something more personal when you asked about God speaking to me."

"Yes, I also had in mind the ways in which God can speak more directly to us. How else do you think God might speak?"

"I'm not sure. Sometimes, though, things happen in my life that I think must have been organised by God—things that can't be just coincidence."

"But God also speaks in other ways too."

"Such as?"

"Have you ever felt any special times when God has been particularly close to you?"

"Yes, sometimes when I have been outside in nature, especially when in the mountains, and I look up at the stars at night, I feel that God is so great and I just stand in awe of him."

"That's wonderful. Certainly God does speak though nature. His creation points us to the fact that there is a Creator who designed it all. Has God spoken to you in any other way?"

"Hmm... there is something, but it's difficult to explain."

"Are you willing to try?"

"I've not told anyone else about this before, not even my wife, because I don't really understand what it means. However, I keep having a dream in which I see a prophet dressed in old-fashioned clothing, but his clothes are shining white. He seemed to be beckoning me as if he wanted me to follow him."

"That's very interesting. Certainly God is speaking to you through your dreams."

"This prophet seems to be so kind and good but I don't know who this prophet is."

"Maybe the holy scriptures could help us. Could I read a description of a great prophet who was seen in a vision given to another man?"

"Please do."

I opened the Holy Book and began to read:

> I turned around to see the voice that was speaking to me. And when I turned I saw seven golden lampstands, and among the lampstands was someone "like a son of man"

dressed in a robe reaching down to his feet and with a golden sash round his chest...[305]

"Yes!" interrupted Vasif, "the prophet in my dream had a golden sash around his chest! Who is this prophet?"

"Let me read a little more," I replied, "and see if any other details match what you saw: 'His head and hair were white like wool, as white as snow, and his eyes were like blazing fire. His feet were like bronze glowing in a furnace, and his voice was like the sound of rushing waters. In his right hand he held seven stars, and out of his mouth came a sharp double-edged sword. His face was like the sun shining in all its brilliance.'[306] What do you think about that description?"

"Some of it matches very well, especially the bit about the shining white clothes, but not the part about the sword in his mouth."

"I think that part is probably symbolic rather than literal and refers to the word of God. Elsewhere in the Holy Books it is written: 'The word of God is living and active. Sharper than any double-edged sword, it penetrates even to dividing soul and spirit, joints and marrow; it judges the thoughts and attitudes of the heart. Nothing in all creation is hidden from God's sight. Everything is uncovered and laid bare before the eyes of him to whom we must give account.'"[307]

"That makes sense to me about the sword being symbolic of the word of God, but what you then read about 'the eyes of him to whom we must give account' makes me think very much of the eyes of the prophet I saw in my dream. I can't describe his eyes but it seemed to me as if he could see right into my heart."

"And how did you feel when you felt that he could look right into your heart?"

"Strangely, I felt loved and accepted. It was as if the prophet understands and loves me, despite all my dirt and darkness inside me."

"Maybe that gives you a clue about who this prophet is."

"The only one I have heard about who really loves and accepts people is Isa Mesih."

"Do you know something else? It is written about Isa Mesih that he 'did not need man's testimony about man, for he knew what was in a man.'[308] The description I just read to you from the *Injil* was of Isa Mesih after he had returned to heaven."

"I'll tell you something else," commented Vasif. "In my dream it was not as if I was hearing spoken words but in my heart I felt as if words were being communicated to me. It was as if the prophet were saying to me, 'I am the way. Follow me'."

"Vasif, it is certainly Isa Mesih who is calling you to follow him. Let me read to you some other words that Isa Mesih said. He said, 'I am the way and the truth and the life. No-one comes to the Father except through me.'"[309]

"If Isa Mesih has been speaking to me through my dreams, what else can I do but to do as he says? He is the prophet who knows everything about me but still loves and accepts me. If he is beckoning to me and if he is the Way, surely I must follow."

THE MOUNTAIN
OF GOD

In the courtyard outside Vasif's house, tied up to a tree opposite the front door, was a sheep. Vasif explained that they had bought the sheep in preparation for the great feast when they sacrifice a sheep and share its meat with neighbours or with poor people.

"Yes, isn't that the feast which is called Kurban Bayram?" I asked.

"That's right. In Azeri we call it Qurban Bayramı, although the Tatars say 'Korban Bayram'. I think in Arabic it is called the Feast of 'Id or the Eid-Ul-Adha."

"Can you tell me more about the meaning of the Feast?"

"What I know is that the prophet Ibrahim was going to offer his own son as a sacrifice. However, at the last minute God spoke to the prophet and told him not to kill his son because God himself was providing a substitute. The prophet looked up and saw a ram caught in a bush, which he then offered instead. That is why we now remember this event by sacrificing a sheep."

"You are obviously well acquainted with the holy books. Why do you think this event is so important that even now, thousands of years later, it is still commemorated by millions of people?"

"I suppose that it is because God does not want human sacrifice, like some pagan peoples did."

"You may well be right there, but I think there is an even deeper meaning."

"What is that?"

"The important fact is that God provided a substitute. It meant that the prophet's son did not have to die. It is this truth that is so important for each one of us because each of us is like the prophet Ibrahim's son."

"How are we like the prophet's son?"

"Do you know anyone who has never sinned?"

"No—all of us are sinners in some way."

"Exactly! But sin leads to death. When the first man, Adam, sinned, it meant that he became mortal and would one day die. It is written in the holy book that 'the wages of sin is death'.[310] It means not only physical death but also eternal separation from God in hell. So that is why we are all destined for death, like the prophet Ibrahim's son was going to die—but then God himself provided a substitute."

"But who or what can substitute for our sin? Can this sheep take away my sin?"

"If this sheep could take away your sin, why do you sacrifice again and again every year?"

"Because I keep on sinning year after year!"

"All of us do! That is why an animal cannot be a perfect sacrifice which is enough for all time. An animal cannot fully take away the sin of a human being. Neither can another imperfect, sinful human being die on behalf of another person because each of us has sin of our own. Dirty water cannot wash away dirt: clean water is needed!"

"So where can we find a clean and pure sacrifice?"

"Only someone without sin can become a pure sacrifice on behalf of someone who is sinful."

"Could such a sacrifice even exist? Who could be without sin? And even if someone were without sin, who would even think of becoming a sacrifice for others?"

"Only one man was totally without sin—Isa Mesih. Isa Mesih is that perfect sacrifice because only he was without any sin at all. We need a sacrifice which is effective for ever! The passage from the Holy Book I just quoted says that the wages of sin is death, but then it continues with a message of hope. It goes on to say 'but the gift of God is eternal life in Isa Mesih our Lord.'"[311]

"Is that so? Do you mean that he became like the sheep, a sacrifice, because only one who is without sin could take away the sin of someone whose heart is as dirty as mine?"

"Exactly. But we need to ask him to take away our sin. The prophet Ibrahim had a choice: either he could carry on and kill his son or else he could accept the sacrifice that God had provided. It meant untying his own son but then taking the sheep as a substitute. We too have the choice of either trying to do things our own way or else of accepting the free gift of eternal life which God is offering through Isa Mesih."

"A free gift? Is it not dependent on my own good or bad deeds?"

"It is as free as the sheep which God gave the prophet Ibrahim."

"This is wonderful news! I would like to receive such a free gift."

"All you have to do is to ask God for it. Ask God to forgive your sins and tell him that you want to receive instead the perfect sacrifice which God himself has provided in Isa Mesih."

Over breakfast the next morning Vasif asked me another question.

"Yesterday we discussed about the sacrifice which God provided. Where was this? I heard it was on some mountain somewhere but I had also been told that it was in Jerusalem. Who is right?"

"The *Taurat* states that it was on a mountain in the 'region of Moriah'.[312] We know where this mountain was because later the prophet Suleiman built a temple to God 'on Mount Moriah'.[313] Do you know where Suleiman built a temple to God?"

"I thought it was in Jerusalem," replied Vasif.

"That's right! So the place where the prophet Ibrahim was about to sacrifice his son, but where God provided a substitute, was in the region of Jerusalem. It was in this very same location that God provided another sacrifice. God allowed Isa Mesih to be killed as a sacrifice for us at the very place where God had provided a sheep as a substitute for the son of Ibrahim."

"In the very same place! So, just as the prophet's son could go free because the sheep died in his place, we too can be saved because of the death of Isa Mesih!"

"Exactly! That is why, when the prophet Yahya saw Isa Mesih, the prophet Yahya said about him, 'Look, the Lamb of God, who takes away the sin of the world!'"[314]

Vasif pondered these words for a while and then made a profound comment.

"That means that Mount Moriah—that is, Jerusalem—was therefore the mountain of salvation. It seems to me that we often think about the mountain of the law, where God gave his commandments to the prophet Musa, but surely we need to focus more on the mountain of salvation. We sacrifice our sheep year after year but we do not know the meaning of what we are doing."

"It was rather like that at the time of Isa Mesih too! The Jews said that the people of Samaria did not worship God on the 'proper' mountain. A Samaritan woman asked Isa Mesih a question, saying, 'Our fathers worshipped on this mountain, but you Jews claim that the place where we must worship is in Jerusalem.'[315] How do you think Isa Mesih responded to this issue?"

"I don't know. If it were here in the Middle East, it would lead to some kind of a quarrel, I guess!"

"Isa Mesih saw that what is important is not so much *what* we do or *where* we do it, but rather the *attitude of our hearts*. God looks at the heart. So Isa Mesih replied, 'Believe me, woman, a time is coming when you will worship the Father neither on this mountain nor in Jerusalem.'[316] For Isa Mesih, the place of worship was not the important question."

"So what is important?" asked Vasif.

"Isa Mesih went on to reveal a far more important truth. He said, 'Yet a time is coming and has now come when the true worshippers will worship the Father in spirit and truth, for they are the kind of worshippers the Father seeks. God is spirit, and his worshippers must worship in spirit and in truth.'"[317]

Vasif pondered these words, then commented, "So you mean that true worship of God is not a matter of rules about physical matters such as the right place for worship? You mean it is a matter of the heart—whether one's heart is fully dedicated or submitted to the ways of God? In other words, it is a *relationship*, not a set of rules."

∽

In the evening, after a busy day, we were gathered around the fireside and again Vasif began to ask questions.

"If Mount Moriah in Israel was the mountain of salvation, why was it that God gave his commandments to the prophet Musa on Mount Sinai?"

I glanced across at little Sadiq, who was playing with a toy near to the fire.

"How many times have you told Sadiq not to touch the fire or to play with it?" I asked.

"Many times!" replied Vasif, "Usually he is fine but there have been times when he has gone too close."

"Maybe that is the answer to your question," I replied. "God loves us, like you love Sadiq, but that is why you also give Sadiq good rules so he does not hurt himself. On Mount

Sinai God gave his special laws to the prophet Musa—the most famous of which are the Ten Commandments. These tell us how to honour God and how to respect other people—including their family life and property. At Mount Sinai God gave many other laws to the prophet Musa. However, the essence of these laws was summed up by Isa Mesih when he was asked which are the greatest commandments. Isa answered that the most important commandment 'is this: "Hear, O Israel, the Lord our God, the Lord is one. Love the Lord your God with all your heart and with all your soul and with all your mind and with all your strength." The second is this: "Love your neighbour as yourself." There is no commandment greater than these.'"[318]

"So again it is what I said this morning," commented Vasif. "What is most important is a relationship with God."

"You are right, Vasif," I replied. "It is like the relationships within a family—between parents and children, or even between a husband and wife. That is why the Holy Books sometimes speak of our relationship with God as being like that of a bride awaiting the bridegroom. It is as if God has paid the *kalym* in Isa Mesih and now God is preparing the bride to be with him for eternity. The final goal of God's plan is a *community*. That community is the 'Holy City, the new Jerusalem, coming down out of heaven from God, prepared as a bride beautifully dressed for her husband.'"[319]

"So the mountain on which the prophet Ibrahim offered his sacrifice, and the mountain where Isa Mesih died for our sins, is not the end, but the beginning?"

"I suppose you could express it that way. Yes, the ultimate place of salvation–the heavenly city–is a *community* of those who know God and are known by God."

"Is that the place to which you are going on pilgrimage?"

"In one way, yes, but all of us are called to go on the pilgrimage to the eternal city."

"Didn't you also say to me that you were on your way to a holy mountain? I thought you meant a mountain here in the Caucasus."

"Actually, there is a holy mountain somewhere around here but I cannot be sure which one it is."

"What do you mean?"

"Somewhere in this part of the world is the place where, after the Great Flood, the large ship carrying the prophet Nuh and his family came to rest on a mountain."

"I thought that was Mount Ararat, which is now on the eastern border of Turkey."

"Many people think that, and it might well be the actual mountain. However, the *Taurat* says that the prophet's large ship came to rest on 'the mountains of Ararat.'"[320]

"Did you say 'mountains'—plural—and not 'mountain'? I know where Mount Ararat is but where are the 'mountains of Ararat'?"

"Maybe not too far away from us now!" I opened my Bible and read from a book of historical events which mentions about the death of the Assyrian king Sennacherib in the seventh century B.C. It is recorded that he was killed by his sons Adrammelech and Sharezer, who then escaped 'to the land of Ararat'.[321] I then explained to Vasif, "What the Hebrews called 'Ararat' was not just the name of a mountain but was also a political term for a country which in the Assyrian records was called Urartu. The prophet Jeremiah also refers to Ararat as a kingdom—one powerful enough to help to destroy the city of Babylon."[323]

"I have heard of Urartu," remarked Vasif. "It was in this part of the Caucasus, though I thought it was more in the region of Armenia and where Mount Ararat is nowadays."

"The problem is," I continued, "that the Great Flood was long before the time of the prophet Jeremiah, so the boundaries of Urartu in his day may not have been anything like the limits of what were called the 'mountains of Ararat' at the time of the prophet Nuh. It was in the ninth century B.C. that the ancient kingdom of Urartu expanded north into the Caucasus—but the prophet Nuh lived a long time before that. In the *Taurat* the exact pronunciation of the region where Nuh's Ark came to rest is not given, because ancient Hebrew (like Classical Arabic) did not use vowels, only consonants. The *Taurat* gives the name of the region in Hebrew as 'rrt'—which could be a rendering either of 'Ararat' or of 'Urartu'. Sumerian sources mention a land called Aratta but its location is unknown. (One Sumerian epic, the epic of Gilgamesh, also contains an account of a great flood.)[323] So we cannot be absolutely certain that the Ark came to rest on what is nowadays called Mount Ararat but it would have been somewhere in this part of the world."

"But Mount Ararat is certainly the biggest and most impressive mountain around here, so it's likely to have been on that mountain anyway!" replied Vasif. "In any case," he continued, "there is a region between Turkey and Armenia which Stalin allotted to Azerbaijan but which still has its Armenian name of Nakhichevan. Apparently in Armenian the name means the original settlement or place of descent where the prophet Nuh and his family first settled when they came out of the Ark."[324]

"If they are right, then it means that the prophet lived in what is now part of Azerbaijan!"

"I'd never thought of it that way before!" replied Vasif. "I always tended to think that he lived in Armenia!"

"Actually, I wouldn't be surprised if he also moved to Georgia!" I added.

"Why do you say that?"

"Often we think of the prophet Nuh as a great hero but the *Taurat* is realistic about even great men of God and also mentions things about them which are not so good. Not many people know that the prophet Nuh made wine and even became drunk!"[325]

"So you think he was the one who started the vineyards of Georgia?"

"Maybe. Around here, Georgia is the most famous region for wine production. Although the words for 'wine' in many languages are based on the Latin *vinum* or Greek *oinos*, in Georgia I was told that some scholars consider that the Romans and Greeks probably derived their words for 'wine' from the Georgian word *ğvino*. Moreover, 'archaeological evidence suggests that the earliest production of wine, made by fermenting grapes, took place in sites in Israel, Georgia and Iran.'"[326]

"If the prophet Nuh also lived in Georgia, maybe his ship came to rest in the mountains of the North Caucasus rather than on what we call Mount Ararat today?"

"Perhaps, but it is speculative. Nowadays it is probably impossible to know for certain. However, the important thing is not the location of the mountain but its spiritual significance. It is like we were discussing this morning."

"So what is the spiritual significance of the mountain where the prophet Nuh's ship came to rest?"

"It was a new beginning. Even though the old world had been destroyed by the great flood, God had rescued enough people and animals to start again."

"I'd not thought of it that way before: the mountain of the prophet Nuh was the mountain of new beginnings. So we have the mountain of the law in the Arabian peninsular—Mount Sinai, the mountain of Musa.[327] Further north, in Israel, actually in Jerusalem, there is the mountain of salvation—the mountain of Ibrahim and also the mountain of Isa Mesih. However, even further north, here in the Caucasus region, we have the mountain of the prophet Nuh, the mountain of new beginnings!"

"I'd not thought of it that way before either!" I remarked.

Vasif was excited by his new train of thought. He went on to say: "In our modern world there are many who say that we need to focus on the mountain of the law. Others say we should focus on the mountain of salvation. Perhaps it is time for all of us to make a new start in our relationships with one another and with God. In our spiritual lives we all need to make, figuratively speaking, a pilgrimage to the mountain of new beginnings."

"I think you are right, Vasif," I agreed. "All of us need to make a fresh start in life. But the problem is that we cannot change ourselves from the inside. Only the power from outside, the power of God himself, is able to give us a new start."

Vasif thought for a moment about this. He was excited about the idea of a mountain of new beginnings but it seemed that he was beginning to wonder how in practical terms the new beginning could come about. Finally, he asked, "How is it that God can give us a new start? How can God change us on the inside? What does this involve?"

In reply I quoted the words of Isa Mesih, who said, "unless a person is born from above, he cannot see the kingdom of God."[328]

"How can a man be born from above?" queried Vasif.

"The religious leader to whom Isa Mesih addressed these words did not understand what Isa Mesih was talking about either! He asked Isa Mesih how a man can be born when he is old.[329] In reply, Isa Mesih said, 'I tell you the truth, no-one can enter the kingdom of God unless he is born of water and the Spirit. Flesh gives birth to flesh, but the Spirit gives birth to spirit.'"[330]

"Are you talking about the passage in the Qur'an which describes how Isa Mesih was born of a specially chosen virgin?[331]" asked Vasif, "Or is this a new relationship with God that all of us can experience? How can we be born of the Spirit, from above?"

"It is something for all of us—or, at least, for all those who want to receive it. It is true that Isa Mesih was born physically in a special and unique way. The angel who announced this news to Marium, the virgin mother of Isa Mesih, explained how it would happen. He said, 'The Holy Spirit will come upon you, and the power of the Most High will overshadow you.'[332] In this way, Isa Mesih had a special relationship with God. However, Isa Mesih also said that each of us needs to be born from above in our spirits in order to enter the kingdom of God. The Spirit gives birth to spirit."

"Who is this Spirit?" asked Vasif.

"He is the Holy Spirit of God. He is the one who was active in the original creation of the universe.[333] If we now receive God's Holy Spirit in our lives, we can become a new creation—like being born from above. He imparts to us a new quality in our relationship with God. It is written that when we receive Isa Mesih, we can also receive God's Holy Spirit to live in us and to make us into people who have a special relationship with God, like that of a parent and child. It is written in the Holy Book that, to all who received Isa Mesih, to those who believed in his name, 'he gave the right to become children of God—children born not of natural descent, nor of human decision or a husband's will, but born of God.'"[334]

"I want to become a child of God," replied Vasif, "I want to receive this Holy Spirit."

"In that case, all you have to do is to talk to God in your own words and ask him to make you new in your spirit. You could say something like the following:

'Holy God, I want to start again in my spiritual life. I realise that I have been trying to do things my own way, and have made a mess of things. I want you to take over and to make me into a child of yours, so that I can hear what you are saying and in that way live my life by your plan and agenda, not in my own way. I am sorry for all the wrong things I have done. Thank you that Isa Mesih died for me as a pure, holy sacrifice. Like the prophet Ibrahim accepting the sheep

231

that you provided, I accept the substitute you have given as a sacrifice for my sin. I'm now coming to the place of new beginnings. I've been trying to live only according the mountain of the law but now I also want to receive what you give at the mountain of salvation. Please send your Holy Spirit to make me clean inside and to give me a new start in my life."

Notes

1. *Injil*: Matthew 1:21, New International Version.

2. See:

   http://www.china.org.cn/english/kuaixun/74860.htm

   http://en.wikipedia.org/wiki/Mogao_Caves

   http://www.chinamuseums.com/dunhuang_mogao.htm

   http://en.wikipedia.org/wiki/Buddhas_of_Bamyan

   http://weekly.ahram.org.eg/2001/565/11wa1.htm

   (all accessed 4 Apr. 2009)

3. *Historical Background Of Buddhism In Afghanistan*

   http://www.4ui.com/eart/144eart1.htm ; see also

   http://www.britannica.com/EBchecked/topic/83184/

   Buddhism/68669/Central-Asia-and-China (both

   accessed 4 Apr. 2009)

4. *Injil*: Acts 2:9. The events of that chapter took place at
   the Jewish festival of Shavuot—alternatively known
   as the Feast of Weeks—which was seven weeks after
   the Passover Festival. It was just before the Passover
   Festival that Isa Mesih was killed but he rose again
   from the dead just after that festival.

   For a map of Parthia at its greatest extent, see http://
   www.parthia.com/map_extent.htm (acc. 16 Sep. 2009).
   Besides this evidence from the Injil, 'there are also ancient traditions that the apostles Thomas and Andrew
   preached to various ancient peoples resident in the
   Persian Empire, including some who lived in Central
   Asia, such as the Bactrians, Scythians, and Sogdians.'

(Mark Dickens, Nestorian Christianity In Central Asia http://www.oxuscom.com/Nestorian_Christianity_in_CA.pdf acc. 19 Sep. 2009, p. 1.)

5. Farida Mamedova *Christianity in Caucasian Albania* http://www.visions.az/history,150 (acc. 22 Apr. 2011)

6. Рашид Азизов, *Табасаранцы: кто они?* [Rashid Azizov, *The Tabassarans: Who are they?*] (Kazan: Zaman publishers, 2002), p. 10

7. Zurab Konanchev, *Udins Today* http://azer.com/aiweb/categories/magazine/ai113_folder/113_articles/113_udins_konanchev.html (acc. 22 Apr. 2011)

8. *East of the Euphrates: Early Christianity in Asia* by T.V. Philip, Chapter 8, *Christianity In Other Places In Asia* http://www.religion-online.org/showchapter.asp?title=1553&C=1365 (acc. 16 Sep. 2009); http://www.newworldencyclopedia.org/entry/Nestorian_Christianity (acc. 19 Sep. 2009); http://www.touchstonemag.com/archives/article.php?id=20-03-030-f (acc. 19 Sep. 2009); Mark Dickens *Nestorian Christianity In Central Asia* http://www.oxuscom.com/Nestorian_Christianity_in_CA.pdf, pp. 1–6. (acc. 19 Sep. 2009)

9. Манарбек Байеке *История Христианства в Центральной Азии и в Казахстане* [Manarbek Baieke *The History of Christianity in Central Asia and Kazakhstan*] (Almaty, 2009), p. 131

10. Mark Dickens *Nestorian Christianity In Central Asia* http://www.oxuscom.com/Nestorian_Christianity_in_CA.pdf, p. 5. (acc. 19 Sep. 2009)

11. http://en.wikipedia.org/wiki/Sogdiana http://east-asian-history.suite101.com/article.cfm/the_sogdians (both accessed 19 Sep. 2009)

12. Mark Dickens *Nestorian Christianity In Central Asia* http://www.oxuscom.com/Nestorian_Christianity_in_CA.pdf, p. 5 (acc. 19 Sep. 2009).

13. Hugh P. Kemp *Steppe by Step* (London: Monarch Books, 2000), pp. 47-118; Mark Dickens *Nestorian Christianity In Central Asia* http://www.oxuscom.com/Nestorian_Christianity_in_CA.pdf, pp. 8–10. (acc. 19 Sep. 2009)

14. *Christianity among the Mongols* http://en.wikipedia.org/wiki/Christianity_among_the_Mongols (acc. 9 Sep. 2009)

15. Mark Dickens *Nestorian Christianity In Central Asia* http://www.oxuscom.com/Nestorian_Christianity_in_CA.pdf, pp. 12–14. (acc. 22 Apr. 2009)

16. Манарбек Байеке *История Христианства в Центральной Азии и в Казахстане* [Manarbek Baieke *The History of Christianity in Central Asia and Kazakhstan*] (Almaty 2009), pp. 300-304; Mark Dickens *Nestorian Christianity In Central Asia* http://www.oxuscom.com/Nestorian_Christianity_in_CA.pdf—with comments on revisions to the text, p.11 (acc. 22 Apr. 2011); http://www.oxuscom.com/graves.htm (acc. 4 Sep. 2009);

http://www.archive.org/stream/MN41565ucmf_1/
MN41565ucmf_1_djvu.txt (acc. 4 Sep. 2009)

17. See the photograph of this tombstone on the
website *Christianity among the Mongols,* http://
en.wikipedia.org/wiki/Christianity_among_the_Mon-
gols. (acc. 9 Sep. 2009)

18. Illustrations of such artifacts are contained in
the book by Manarbek Baieke entitled *История
Христианства в Центральной Азии и в
Казахстане* [*The History of Christianity in Central
Asia and Kazakhstan*] (Almaty, 2009), and can be
seen, for example, on pages 134, 173, 178 and 291.

19. Манарбек Байеке *История Христианства в
Центральной Азии и в Казахстане* [Manarbek
Baieke *The History of Christianity in Central Asia
and Kazakhstan*] (Almaty, 2009); Farida Mamedova
Christianity in Caucasian Albania http://www.
visions.az/history,150 (acc. 22 Apr. 2011);
Рашид Азизов *Традиционная духовная культура
Табасарана XIX-XX вв.* [Rashid Azizov *The
Traditional spiritual culture of the Tabassarans in the
19th–20th centuries*] (Makhachkala, 2007)

20. http://www.crc-internet.org/CCR/2009/77-Saint-
Thomas_China.php (acc. 6 Jun. 2011)

21. http://www.christianityinchina.org/Common/Admin/
showNews_auto.jsp?Nid=304 ; *Christian Designs Found
in Tomb Stones of Eastern Han Dynasty*
http://www.chinaartnetworks.com/news/show_news.
php?id=1369 (both accessed 20 Apr. 2011)

22. *Nestorian Christianity in the Tang Dynasty* http://
     www.orthodox.cn/localchurch/jingjiao/nest1.htm ;
     http://ricci.rt.usfca.edu/hist3.html (both
     accessed 20 Apr. 2011)

23. At that time the city was called Chang'an and was the
     capital of the Tang Dyanasty. The Nestorian Stele can
     be seen on display in room number two of the 'Forest
     of Steles' Museum (西安碑林博物館—Xi'an Beilin
     Bowuguan) in Xi'an (西安).

     http://www.absoluteastronomy.com/topics/Nesto-
     rian_Stele#encyclopedia

     For further information see also
     http://www.aina.org/articles/dasotns.pdf
     http://www.cf.ac.uk/clarc/projects/chinesenesto-
     rian/index.html
     http://www.statemaster.com/encyclopedia/Nestori-
     anism-in-China
     http://www.usfca.edu/ricci/christianity/index.htm
     http://wapedia.mobi/en/Nestorian_Stele
     http://www.reference.com/browse/wiki/Nesto-
     rian_Stele
     http://www.statemaster.com/encyclopedia/
     Nestorian-Stele
     http://en.wikipedia.org/wiki/Nestorian_Stele
     (all accessed 19 Sep. 2009)

24. http://www.crystalinks.com/chinacaves.html
     http://en.wikipedia.org/wiki/Dunhuang (both
     accessed 20 Apr. 2011)

25. Patrick Johnstone *The Church is bigger than you
     think* (Fearn, Scotland: Christian Focus Publications,
     1998), p. 73. Kenny Joseph and his son of the same

name believe that Christianity had also reached Japan in the same period: their reasons are presented, in Japanese, in their book 十字架の国—日本 [*Jujika no kuni—Nihon*] (Tokyo: Tokuma Shoten, 2000).

26.   Philip Jenkins *The Lost History of Christianity: The Thousand-Year Golden Age of the Church in the Middle East, Africa, and Asia—and How It Died* (Harper One publishers, 2008); 'Christianity's Lost History: Recovering a Forgotten Chapter' http://www.aina.org/ata/20090429174105.htm; T.V. Philip, *East Of The Euphrates: Early Christianity In Asia* http://www.religion-online.org/showchapter.asp?title=1553&C=1368 (both accessed 4 Sep. 2009)

27.   Рашид Азизов *Традиционная духовная культура Табасарана XIX-XX вв.* [Rashid Azizov *Traditional spiritual culture of the Tabassarans in the nineteenth and twentieth centuries*] (Makhachkala, 2007), p. 120

28.   *ibid*, p. 123 [The name translated into English as 'Halah' is rendered as 'Khalakh' (Халах) in the Russian Synodal version of the Bible; Rashid Azizov gives the Tabassaran name of the settlement as 'Khalag'.]

29.   http://www.bethelcog.org/church/the-origin-of-our-western-heritage/the-captivity-and-deportation-of-israel
      http://en.wikipedia.org/wiki/Assyrian_captivity_of_Israel
      http://www.ucgstp.org/lit/booklets/usbbp/ch3nkingdom.html
      http://www.ucg.org/booklets/US/northernkingdom.asp (all accessed 10 Sep. 2009)

30. The Tabassaran people of Dagestan are also thought to have had Jewish origins, according to sources cited by Rashid Azizov on pages six and seven of his booklet *'The Tabassarans: Who are they?'*. (Kazan: Zaman publishers, 2002). [See Рашид Азизов *Табасаранцы: кто они?* (Казань: Издательство «Заман», 2002, citing Г.-Э. Авкарди *Ассари Дагестан* (Махачкала, 1929, с. 13) and also the author of *Очерк Кайтаго-Табасаранского округа* (Кавказ, 1867, №. 7).]

31. Манарбек Байеке *История Христианства в Центральной Азии и в Казахстане* [Manarbek Baieke *The History of Christianity in Central Asia and Kazakhstan*] (Almaty, 2009) pp. 33–34;

    http://www.britannica.com/EBchecked/topic/530361/Scythian

    http://en.wikipedia.org/wiki/Scythians

    http://en.wikipedia.org/wiki/Sakas

    http://www.livius.org/sao-sd/scythians/scythians.html (all accessed 22 Apr. 2011)

32. http://en.wikipedia.org/wiki/Khazars#Khazar_religion

    http://www.khazaria.com/khazar-history.html

    http://www.doingzionism.org.il/resources/view.asp?id=140

    Paul Meerts *Assessing Khazaria* (I.I.A.S. Newsletter, number 34, July 2004) http://www.iias.nl/nl/34/IIAS_NL34_15.pdf (all accessed 22 Sep. 2009)

33. http://en.wikipedia.org/wiki/Khazars#Khazar_religion

    http://www.khazaria.com/khazar-history.html

    Paul Meerts *Assessing Khazaria* (I.I.A.S. Newsletter,

number 34, July 2004) http://www.iias.nl/nl/34/
IIAS_NL34_15.pdf (all accessed 23 Sep. 2009)

34. *Taurat*: Exodus 3:6, New International Version.

35. http://en.wikipedia.org/wiki/Nasreddin
http://www.allaboutturkey.com/nasreddin.htm (both
accessed 5 Sep. 2009)

36. http://en.wikipedia.org/wiki/Nasreddin (acc. 5 Sep.
2009), quoting Idris Shah *The Sufis* (London: W. H.
Allen, 1964).

37. *Injil*: Luke 18:38, NET Bible.

38. *Injil*: Luke 18:41, NET Bible.

39. *Taurat*: Deuteronomy 8:3, New International Version.

40. *Injil*: Matthew 4:4; Luke 4:4.

41. Qur'an sura 10 (Jonah): 94, cited from M.H. Shakir's
searchable translation of the Qur'an at http://etext.
virginia.edu/toc/modeng/public/HolKora.html (acc.
17 Jan. 2009). [Ali knew that the verse existed but
was unable to quote it word for word so the fuller
text of the verse is given here. In the same way, various
quotations from the *Taurat*, *Zabur* and *Injil* are also
quoted more fully.]

42. *Injil*: 2 Corinthians 3:2, NET Bible.

43. 非常好，非常好

44. *Injil*: 2 Corinthians 9:7, NET Bible.

45. *Injil*: Mark 12:41–44, NET Bible.

46. Taicang yi su (太仓一粟)

47. *Injil*: James 1:27, New International Version.

48. *Taurat*: Genesis 22:11–12, New International Version.

49. *Injil*: John 1:29, NET Bible.

50. *Injil*: 1 Peter 2:22; 1 John 3:5, NET Bible.

51. *Injil*: John 8:46, NET Bible.

52. In the Qur'an (3:45) Isa Mesih is called *kalimatullah* (the word of God). The passages in the Injil are given below.

53. *Injil*: John 1:1–4, New International Version.

54. *Injil*: John 1:14, New International Version.

55. *Injil*: John 1:10–13, New International Version.

56. *Injil*: Romans 8:31–32, NET Bible.

57. Elza-Bair Guchinova *The Kalmyks* (London and New York: Routledge, 2006), pp. 214-215

58. For information on the Hazara people, see, for example:
    http://en.wikipedia.org/wiki/Hazara_people
    http://www.hazara.net
    http://www.britannica.com/EBchecked/topic/257908/Hazara
    Some information on the Mongolians of Yunnan province is available at: http://english.cnyntour.com/printpage.asp?ArticleID=3810
    http://en.wikipedia.org/wiki/Yunnan_Mongols

http://www.paulnoll.com/China/Minorities/min-Mongolian.html
http://www.hamagmongol.narod.ru/splinters/myunnan_e.htm (all accessed 26 Jan. 2010)

59. Ecclesiastes 1:11, New International Version.

60. *Injil*: John 5:5–6, New International Version.

61. *Injil*: Matthew 6:16–18 , NET Bible.

62. *Injil*: Luke 4:2, NET Bible.

63. *Injil*: Matthew 4:4, New International Version.

64. Isaiah 58:3–7, New International Version.

65. *Injil*: Matthew 22:37–40, New International Version.

66. *Injil*: Luke 15:11–32, New International Version.

67. *Taurat*: Genesis 6:5–6, New International Version.

68. *Injil*: Philippians 2:3–8, New International Version.

69. *Injil*: John 4:14, New International Version.

70. *Injil*: John 7:37b-39a, New International Version.

71. *Taurat*: Genesis chapter 41

72. *Injil*: Matthew 27:19, New International Version.

73. *Injil*: Matthew 6:9–13, NET Bible.

74. *Injil*: Luke 17:26–30, New International Version.

75. Joel 2:30–32a, NET Bible.

76. Joel 2:28–29, NET Bible.

77. *Injil*: Acts chapter 2

78. *Injil*: 1 Timothy 2:5–6, NET Bible.

79. http://www.newworldencyclopedia.org/entry/Nesto-
    rian_Christianity
    http://www.statemaster.com/encyclopedia/
    Nestorian-Stele
    http://www.absoluteastronomy.com/topics/Assyr-
    ian_Church_of_the_East_in_China
    http://www.touchstonemag.com/archives/article.
    php?id=20-03-030-f (all accessed 28 Nov. 2009)

80. Although there were some Muslims in China during
    the Tang dynasty, they were mainly Arab and Persian
    merchants living in larger cities such as Guangzhou,
    Hangzhou or Chang'an (http://en.wikipedia.org/
    wiki/Islam_in_China, acc. 28 Nov. 2009).

81. http://en.wikipedia.org/wiki/Shangdi (acc. 1 July
    2008); Chan Kei Thong *Faith of Our Fathers: God in
    Ancient China* (Shanghai, China: China Publishing
    Group Orient Publishing Center, 2006), pp. 79-106

82. *Injil*: Matthew 20:1–16

83. *Injil*: Romans 12:13, New International Version.

84. *Injil*: 1 Peter 4:9, New International Version.

85. *Injil*: Hebrews 13:2, New International Version.

86. *Taurat*: Genesis 18: 1–14, NET Bible.

87. *Taurat*: Exodus 16: 4–5, 13–18, 21–31, 35, NET
    Bible.

88. *Injil*: John 6: 1–13, NET Bible.

89. *Injil*: John 6: 26–40, NET Bible.

90. Isaiah 25:6, New International Version.

91. *Injil*: Matthew 8:11, New International Version.

92. *Injil*: Revelation 3:20, New International Version.

93. *Taurat*: Genesis 15:5

94. Once when I was in Dagestan a Kumyk man had offered another explanation, about it being for hygienic purposes.

95. My speech on that occasion was briefer than that given here but contained the same main points. I have taken the liberty of expanding here on some of the points and going into a little more detail.

96. *Taurat*: Genesis 11:31 'The most generally-accepted theory at the present time is that Ur is to be identified with the modern Mugheir (or Mughayyar, "the pitchy") in Southern Babylonia, called Urumma, or Urima, and later Uru in the inscriptions.' (http://bibleatlas.org/ur.htm). Its location in modern-day Iraq is shown on a map available at http://www.traveljournals.net/explore/iraq/map/m4398374/ur_of_the_chaldees.html.

     However, there are other possible sites which have been suggested as locations of the ancient city of Ur. Some writers argue that that it was somewhere in what is now 'south-central Turkey, near the Syrian border' (http://members.bib-arch.org/search.asp?PubID=BSBA&Volume=3&Issue=2&ArticleID=5&User

ID=0&) or else in the region of the mountains of Ararat
(http://home.clara.net/arlev/genabraham.htm),
probably on the present-day borderlands between
Turkey and Armenia. These writers argue that it was
in any case located far to the north of Iraq. Perhaps
there is even a possibility that the prophet might have
lived somewhere in what is now the Caucasus region
or Central Asia. (All accessed 30 Nov. 2009)

97. *Taurat*: Genesis 12:1–3, New International Version.

98. *Taurat*: Genesis 11:31. Haran was near to the modern
city of Urfa in south-east Turkey. See, for example:
http://www.bible-history.com/maps/patrarch_wan-
derings.html
http://www.traveljournals.net/explore/turkey/map/
m1075308/haran.html
http://www.greek-language.com/bible/
palmer/04geohist.html (all accessed 30 Nov. 2009)

99. *Taurat*: Genesis 12:4–7, NET Bible.

100. *Taurat*: Genesis 15:2–5, New International Version.

101. *Taurat*: Genesis 15:6, New International Version.

102. *Taurat*: Genesis 16:1–4, New International Version.

103. *Taurat*: Genesis 16:15, New International Version.

104. *Taurat*: Genesis 17:1b–2, NET Bible.

105. *Taurat*: Genesis 17:4–8, NET Bible.

106. *Injil*: Ephesians 2:8–9, NET Bible.

107. *Taurat*: Genesis 17:9–16, New International Version.

108. *Taurat*: Genesis 17:17–18, New International Version.

109. *Taurat*: Genesis 17:19–21, New International Version.

110. *Taurat*: Genesis 17:23–27, New International Version.

111. Jeremiah 9:25–26, New International Version.

112. See the *Injil*: Colossians 2:11

113. *Injil*: Romans 4:11–12, NET Bible.

114. *Injil*: 1 Corinthians 7:19, NET Bible.

115. *Injil*: Galatians 6:15, NET Bible.

116. *Injil*: Matthew 28:20, New International Version.

117. *Injil*: John 16:7, New International Version.

118. *Injil*: John 14:16–18, New International Version.

119. *Injil*: Acts 16:7

120. *Injil*: John 14:26, New International Version.

121. http://members.tripod.com/~khorasan/Miscellane-ous/aspand.html quoted on the website http://www.luckymojo.com/aspand.html, acc. 15 July 2008. (I have been unable to access the original website.) The prayer is also given on the website http://tajikam.com/index.php?option=com_content&task=view&id=56&Itemid=37 (acc. 21 Dec. 2011) These sources give the name as 'aspand' but the Tajik spelling испанд is better transliterated as *ispand*. Its Latin name is *Peganum*

harmala and it is known in English as harmal
or as 'Syrian rue': for further details, see http://
en.wikipedia.org/wiki/Harmal. (acc. 21 Dec. 2011)

122. http://www.luckymojo.com/aspand.html (acc. 15 July
2008); http://herb-magic.com/aspand.html (acc. 21
Dec. 2011)

123. Job 3:25, New International Version.

124. Job 1:4–5, New International Version.

125. Job 42:1–6, New International Version.

126. *Injil*: Matthew 6:25–34, New International Version.

127. *Zabur*: Psalm 111:10, New International Version.

128. Proverbs 9:10, New International Version.

129. Proverbs 1:7, New International Version.

130. *Taurat*: Genesis 3:15, New International Version.

131. *Injil*: Matthew 10:8; Mark 16:17; Acts 16:18; Philippians 2:9–10 etc.

132. *Injil*: Romans 8:38–39, New International Version.

133. *Injil*: 1 John 4:16b-18, New International Version.

134. See the *Injil*: John 10:10.

135. Job 1:1–3, New International Version.

136. See Lamentations 4:21 and Jeremiah 25:20; compare
also the names mentioned in Genesis 10:23, 22:21
and 36:28 as well as 1 Chronicles 1:17.

137. Job 1:6–12, New International Version.

138. Job 1:18–19, New International Version.

139. See Job 1:13–17.

140. *Injil*: Luke 8:22–25

141. Job 1:20–22, New International Version.

142. Job 2:1–10, New International Version.

143. *Injil*: John 9:1–7, NET Bible.

144. *Injil*: Matthew 9:35–36, NET Bible.

145. Job 42:3

146. Job 42:7b, New International Version.

147. Job 19:25–27, New International Version.

148. *Injil*: Titus 2:11–14, NET Bible.

149. *Injil*: Mark 10:45, NET Bible.

150. Daniel 7:13–14, New International Version.

151. *Injil*: John 18:36

152. *Injil*: Matthew 26:63–66, New International Version. (See also Luke 22:67–71)

153. 1 Chronicles 17:11–14, New International Version.

154. *Injil*: John 1:49, NET Bible.

155. *Injil*: Mark 15:39, NET Bible. Compare also Matthew 27:54, which mentions about an earthquake that took place at the time Isa Mesih died—and which was a further sign from God about the special nature of Isa Mesih.

156. *Injil*: John 14:9, New International Version.

157. *Injil*: 1 Peter 2:21–23, New International Version.

158. *Injil*: 1 Peter 2:24, New International Version.

159. This was the old border crossing. Nowadays the border crossing is in a different place.

160. *Taurat*: Genesis 1:27–28, New International Version.

161. "Allah enjoins you concerning your children: The male shall have the equal of the portion of two females; then if they are more than two females, they shall have two-thirds of what the deceased has left, and if there is one, she shall have the half; and as for his parents, each of them shall have the sixth of what he has left if he has a child, but if he has no child and (only) his two parents inherit him, then his mother shall have the third; but if he has brothers, then his mother shall have the sixth after (the payment of) a bequest he may have bequeathed or a debt; your parents and your children, you know not which of them is the nearer to you in usefulness; this is an ordinance from Allah: Surely Allah is Knowing, Wise." (Qur'an 4.11, in M.H. Shakir's searchable translation of the Qur'an at http://www.hti.umich.edu/k/koran, accessed 1 Feb. 2012)

162. "And do not kill your children for fear of poverty; We give them sustenance and yourselves (too); surely to kill them is a great wrong." (17.31) Compare also: "And thus their associates have made fair seeming to most of the polytheists the killing of their children, that they may cause them to perish and obscure for them their religion; and if Allah had pleased, they

would not have done it, therefore leave them and that which they forge." (6.137, in M.H. Shakir's searchable translation of the Qur'an at http://www.hti.umich.edu/k/koran, accessed 1 Feb. 2012)

163. "Wealth and children are an adornment of the life of this world; and the ever-abiding, the good works, are better with your Lord in reward and better in expectation. (18.46, in M.H. Shakir's searchable translation of the Qur'an at http://www.hti.umich.edu/k/koran, accessed 1 Feb. 2012)

164. *Zabur*: Psalm 127:3–5, New International Version.

165. *Zabur*: Psalm 103:13, New International Version.

166. *Injil*: Luke 3:38, New International Version.

167. *Taurat*: Genesis 2:7, New International Version.

168. Malachi 2:10, New International Version.

169. Isaiah 1:2, New International Version.

170. Proverbs 3:11–12, New International Version.

171. *Injil*: Hebrews 12:5–11, New International Version.

172. *Taurat*: Exodus 20:15; *Injil*: Ephesians 4:28

173. *Injil*: Romans 2:14–15, NET Bible.

174. *Injil*: Romans 5:3–5, New International Version.

175. *Injil*: Romans 8:15.

176. *Injil*: Romans 8:14–17, NET Bible.

177. *Injil*: Galatians 5:16–25, New International Version.

178. *Injil*: John 16:7–15, New International Version.

179. *Taurat*: Leviticus 19:32, New International Version.

180. Proverbs 14:29, New International Version.

181. Proverbs 19:11, New International Version.

182. Proverbs 25:15, New International Version.

183. Proverbs 10:4–5, New International Version.

184. Proverbs 12:11, New International Version.

185. Proverbs 6:6–11, New International Version.

186. Proverbs 12:19, New International Version.

187. Proverbs 14:25, New International Version.

188. Proverbs 12:22, New International Version.

189. Proverbs 16:13, New International Version.

190. *Taurat*: Genesis 1:26, New International Version.

191. *Taurat*: Genesis 5:1–3, New International Version.

192. *Taurat*: Exodus 35:30–35, New International Version.

193. *Injil*: 2 Timothy 2:15, New International Version.

194. *Injil*: Colossians 1:13–17, New International Version.

195. *Injil*: John 1:1–3, New International Version.

196. *Injil*: Ephesians 2:10, New International Version.

197. *Injil*: Acts 10:38, New International Version.

198. See the Qur'an sura 3 (The Family of Imran): 49

199. *Injil*: John 6:29, New International Version.

200. Isaiah 53:7, New International Version.

201. *Injil*: Luke 23:32–34, New International Version.

202. Proverbs 8:11, New International Version.

203. *Injil*: James 1:5–8, New International Version.

204. Proverbs 9:10, New International Version.

205. Proverbs 18:22, New International Version.

206. *Injil*: Matthew 6:31–33, New International Version.

207. *Taurat*: Genesis 24:3–4, New International Version.

208. *Taurat*: Genesis 24:12–15, New International Version.

209. *Taurat*: Genesis 24:17–20, New International Version.

210. *Taurat*: Genesis 24:15–16, New International Version.

211. *Taurat*: Genesis 24:58, New International Version.

212. *Taurat*: Genesis 24:53, New International Version.

213. *Injil*: 1 Peter 1:18–19, New International Version.

214. *Injil*: John 15:13–14, New International Version.

215. *Injil*: Titus 3:4–6, New International Version.

216. *Injil*: Ephesians 5:25–33, New International Version.

217. *Injil*: 1 John 4:7–8, 16–19, New International Version.

218. *Taurat*: Genesis 2:18, New International Version.

219. *Injil*: John, 14:26–27, New International Version.

220. *Injil*: Revelation 21:1–4, New International Version.

221. *Injil*: Revelation 22:17, New International Version.

222. *Taurat*: Exodus 20:12, New International Version.

223. *Taurat*: Deuteronomy 8:19–20, 28:58–68

224. *Taurat*: Genesis 17:3–8

225. *Injil*: Matthew 3:7–10, New International Version.

226. *Injil*: John 8:34–44, New International Version.

227. Isaiah 1:2–3, New International Version.

228. Isaiah 63:15–16, New International Version.

229. Malachi 2:10, New International Version.

230. *Injil*: Luke 3:23–38, NET Bible.

231. Isaiah 8:19, New International Version.

232. *Taurat*: Leviticus 19:31, New International Version. Similar teaching is also found in Deuteronomy 18:10–13, which says: 'Let no one be found among you who sacrifices his son or daughter in the fire, who practices divination or sorcery, interprets omens, engages in witchcraft, or casts spells, or who is a medium or spiritist or who consults the dead. Anyone who does these things is detestable to the Lord, and because of these detestable practices the Lord your God will drive out those nations before you.' (New International Version)

233. *Injil*: Matthew 10:8; Mark 16:17; Luke 10:17–20

234. *Injil*: Luke 11:24–26

235. *Taurat*: Leviticus 19:28; Deuteronomy 14:1–2

236. *Taurat*: Deuteronomy 26:13–14

237. *Injil*: Mark 7:9–13, New International Version.

238. See, for example, Nehemiah 7:5–65 for the importance of family records but there are many examples of genealogies elsewhere in the Bible, such as in 1 Chronicles chapters 1 to 9.

239. *Taurat*: Genesis 9:12–17

240. *Injil*: 1 Peter 1:3–5, New International Version.

241. *Injil*: Ephesians 1:13–14, New International Version.

242. *Injil*: Galatians 4:6–7, New International Version.

243. *Injil*: Hebrews 1:1–2, New International Version.

244. *Injil*: Hebrews 9:16–17, New International Version.

245. *Injil*: John 10:14–18, New International Version.

246. *Injil*: Colossians 1:10–12, New International Version.

247. Elza-Bair Guchinova *The Kalmyks* (London and New York: Routledge, 2006), p. 183

248. *ibid.*

249. Proverbs 30:18–19, New International Version.

250. Proverbs 30:24–28, New International Version.

251. Elza-Bair Guchinova, *op. cit.*, p. 183

252. His writings were in German, which is why they were not so well known in other parts of the world. English translations of his main ideas are available in Wilhelm Schmidt *The Origin and Growth of Religion: Facts and Theories*, translated by H. J. Rose (Methuen, London, 1931) and in Wilhelm Schmidt *Primitive Revelation*, translated by Joseph Abierl (St. Louis: R. Herder Publishers, 1939)—the original title of which was *Der Ursprung der Gottesidee* [*The Origin of the Concept of God*], published in 1934.

253. Rafael Bezertinov *Old-Turkic Deities*, from his book *Tengrianizm—Religion Of Túrks And Mongols* (Naberezhnye Chelny, Tatarstan, Russian Federation, 2000), Chapter III *Deities*, pp. 71-95, an English translation of which is available at: http://aton.ttu.edu/OLD_TURK_DEITIES.asp (acc. 21 Nov. 2008)

254. http://wapedia.mobi/en/Shangdi
http://www.newworldencyclopedia.org/entry/Shangdi#Meaning_.26_Use_of_Name
http://en.wikipedia.org/wiki/Tian (all accessed 21 Nov. 2008); Chan Kei Thong *Faith of Our Fathers: God in Ancient China* (Shanghai, China: China Publishing Group Orient Publishing Center, 2006), pp. 79-106

255. http://en.wikipedia.org/wiki/Shangdi (acc. 21 Nov. 2008); Patrick Zukeran *The Origin of Man's Religions* http://www.probe.org/site/c.fdKEIMNsEoG/b.4217657/ (acc. 10 Nov. 2008)

256. Rick Brown *Who was 'Allah' before Islam?* (1)
http://www.themicahmandate.org/2009/03/who-was-%E2%80%98allah%E2%80%99-before-islam-1/ (acc. 15 Feb. 2010)

257. *Taurat*: Exodus 3:13–15, New International Version.

258. 3.42 to 3.55 in M.H. Shakir's searchable translation of the Qur'an at http://www.hti.umich.edu/k/koran (acc. 15 Jan. 2008).

259. *Injil*: Matthew 28:18, New International Version.

260. *Injil*: Matthew 10:1, New International Version.

261. *Injil*: Matthew 10:8, New International Version.

262. Quoted by David Pytches in *Come, Holy Spirit: Learning to Minister in Power* (London: Hodder and Stoughton, 1985), pp. 238-9

263. *Injil*: Luke 8:49–55, New International Version.

264. Quoted by David Pytches in *Come, Holy Spirit: Learning to Minister in Power* (London: Hodder and Stoughton, 1985), pp. 236-7

265. 1 Kings 17:17–24, New International Version.

266. Quoted by David Pytches in *Come, Holy Spirit: Learning to Minister in Power* (London: Hodder and Stoughton, 1985), p. 235

267. *Injil*: John 11:1–3, 17–44, NET Bible.

268. Quoted by Jack Deere *Surprised by the Power of the Spirit: Discovering How God Speaks and Heals Today*

(Zondervan Publishers, 1996), pp. 205-206—quoting Mahesh Chadva *Only Love can make a Miracle* (Tunbridge Wells, England: Monarch Books, 1991).

269. *Injil*: John 14:1–3, New International Version.

270. *Injil*: John 14:4, New International Version.

271. *Injil*: John 14:5, New International Version.

272. *Injil*: John 14:6, New International Version.

273. 46.9 in M.H. Shakir's searchable translation of the Qur'an at http://www.hti.umich.edu/k/koran (acc. 15 Jan. 2008).

274. 6.32 in M.H. Shakir's searchable translation of the Qur'an at http://www.hti.umich.edu/k/koran (accessed 4 Nov. 2006).

275. 7.51 in M. H. Shakir *op. cit.*

276. 29.64 in M. H. Shakir *op. cit.*

277. *Injil*: 1 Timothy 4:8, New International Version.

278. *Injil*: Hebrews 12:1, New International Version.

279. *Injil*: Hebrews 12:2–3, New International Version.

280. *Injil*: John 3:19–21, New International Version.

281. http://www.liza-kliko.com/laurel-wreath/olympic.htm. (acc. 4 Sep. 2006)

282. http://www.liza-kliko.com/laurel-wreath/romanempire.htm. (acc. 4 Sep. 2006)

283. *Injil*: James 1:12, New International Version.

284. *Injil*: 2 Timothy 4:7b–8, New International Version.

285. *Injil*: Revelation 2:10, New International Version.

286. Jeremiah 31:33–34, New International Version.

287. *Injil*: John 14: 26, New International Version.

288. Isaiah 6:1–5, New International Version.

289. In the Qur'an, the prophet Ibrahim's nephew is called Lut (e.g. Sura 15, verses 59 and 61) but in the Hebrew *Taurat* he is called Lot.

290. *Taurat*: Genesis 18:16–22; Genesis 19:1–29. The *Taurat* specifies in Genesis 19:1 that those sent to rescue Lut were angels, even though they looked like ordinary human beings.

291. *Injil*: Hebrews 1:14, New International Version.

292. *Injil*: Revelation 12:7–9, New International Version.

293. *Injil*: 1 John 3:8

294. *Taurat*: Exodus 15:26, New International Version.

295. *Injil*: Matthew 17:1–3, New International Version.

296. *Injil*: Hebrews 1:3b–4, New International Version.

297. *Injil*: Matthew 26:53

298. *Injil*: 1 Peter 3:18–22

299. *Injil*: Hebrews 2:14–16, New International Version.

300. *Injil*: Hebrews 2:9, New International Version.

301. *Zabur*: Psalm 23:1–6, New International Version.

302. *Injil*: John 10:11–15, New International Version.

303. *Injil*: Hebrews 11:8–10, New International Version.

304. *Injil*: Colossians 3:2, New International Version.

305. *Injil*: Revelation 1:12–13, New International Version.

306. *Injil*: Revelation 1:14–16, New International Version.

307. *Injil*: Hebrews 4:12–13, New International Version.

308. *Injil*: John 2:25, New International Version.

309. *Injil*: John 14:6, New International Version.

310. *Injil*: Romans 6:23, New International Version.

311. *Injil*: Romans 6:23, New International Version.

312. *Taurat*: Genesis 22:2, New International Version.

313. 2 Chronicles 3:1, New International Version.

314. *Injil*: John 1:29, New International Version.

315. *Injil*: John 4:20, New International Version.

316. *Injil*: John 4:21, New International Version.

317. *Injil*: John 4:23–24, New International Version.

318. *Injil*: Mark 12:29–31, New International Version.

319. *Injil*: Revelation 21:2, New International Version.

320. *Taurat*: Genesis 8:4, New International Version.

321. 2 Kings 19:37, New International Version.

322. Jeremiah 51:27

323. An early version of this epic dates from the 'Old Baby-
    lonian period' (1800—1600 BC)—that is, several
    hundred years before the political state of Urartu.
    See Maureen Gallery Kovacs *The Epic of Gilgamesh*
    (Stanford University Press, 1989), Introduction p.
    xxii.

324. For an easily available discussion of the etymology of
    the name, see http://en.wikipedia.org/wiki/Nakh-
    chivan. An Azeri source says that it means 'colony of
    Noah' (http://www.azerb.com/az-nakhchivan.html).
    (both accessed 4 Apr. 2009)

325. *Taurat*: Genesis 9:20–21

326. http://www.reference.com/browse/wine (acc. 15 Jan.
    2009)

327. During the time of the Roman Empire, this mountain
    was located in the province called Arabia Petraea or
    Provincia Arabia—a territory which included the
    Sinai peninsula, the north-western part of what is
    now Saudi Arabia and also parts of what are now
    Jordan and Syria (http://en.wikipedia.org/wiki/
    Arabia_Petraea, accessed 15 Jan. 2009). This province
    was also called simply 'Arabia', which is why the Injil,
    written in Roman times, mentions that Mount Sinai
    was in 'Arabia' (*Injil*: Galatians 4:25).

328. *Injil*: John 3:3, NET Bible.

329. *Injil*: John 3:4

330. *Injil*: John 3:5–6, New International Version.

331. Qur'an sura 3 (The Family of Imran):43–47

332. *Injil*: Luke 1:35, New International Version.

333. *Taurat*: Genesis 1:2

334. *Injil*: John 1:12–13, New International Version.

Lightning Source UK Ltd.
Milton Keynes UK
UKOW042054030812

197020UK00004B/6/P